The Defence of the Priesthood

Real View Books

J. H. Newman, *Anglican Difficulties*

A. Carrel, *Voyage to Lourdes*

J. H. De Groot, *The Shakespeares and the "Old Faith"*★

K. A. Kneller, *Christianity and the Leaders of Modern Science*

A. Barruel, *Memoirs Illustrating the History of Jacobinism*

H. E. Manning, *True Story of the Vatican Council*

All titles with an Introduction (★Postscript)
by Stanley L. Jaki

Saint John Fisher

The Defence
of the Priesthood

with an Introduction by

Stanley L. Jaki

Real View Books

Published by
AMERICAN COUNCIL ON ECONOMICS AND SOCIETY
34152 Doreka Drive
Fraser, Michigan 48026

1996

All rights reserved. No part of this publication may be reproduced, stored in a retrieval system, or transmitted in any form, or by any means, electronic, mechanical, photocopying, recording or otherwise, without prior permission of American Council on Economics and Society.

© (Introduction) Stanley L. Jaki

© (Appendix) Anne Barbeau Gardiner

Saint John Fisher, bishop of Rochester (1469?-1535)

1. Theology of the priesthood. 2. Refutation of Luther

ISBN 0-9641150-7-7

Mgr. Philip E. Haller's translation of *The Defence of the Priesthood*, originally published by Burns, Oates & Washbourne (London: 1935), is reprinted here in a facsimile form with the kind permission of Burns & Oates Ltd., Tunbridge Wells, England.

The illustration on the cover shows part of John Fisher's bust made by Torrigiano around 1507, or about three years after Fisher's consecration as a bishop, an office which he held for over thirty years with a saintly dedication to its fulness of the priesthood.

Printed in the United States of America

Contents

Introduction by Stanley L. Jaki		VII–XXIX
Translator's Preface		vii
1. Prologue		1
2. First Rejoinder		4
3. Second Rejoinder. Introduction		22
4.	First Axiom	24
5.	Second Axiom	29
6.	Third Axiom	33
7.	Fourth Axiom	37
8.	Fifth Axiom	41
9.	Sixth Axiom	45
10.	Seventh Axiom	49
11.	Eighth Axiom	53
12.	Ninth Axiom	58
13.	Tenth Axiom	64
14.	Conclusion	74
15. Third Rejoinder. Introduction		77

16.	First Text	83
17.	Second Text	85
18.	Third Text	87
19.	Fourth Text	90
20.	Fifth Text	94
21.	Sixth Text	95
22.	Refutation of Luther's First Attack	97
23.	Refutation of Luther's Second Attack	110
24.	Refutation of Luther's Third Attack	116
25.	Epilogue	138
Notes		139
Index		150
Appendix. Sermon against Luther		151-182

Introduction

The present work is a translation of John Fisher's animated defense of the idea of the priesthood as understood by the Catholic Church. The translator, Mgr. Philip Edward Hallett, was the vice-postulator of the canonization of John Fisher and Sir Thomas More which took place on May 19, 1935. By bringing out this book just a few months before the canonization, Mgr. Hallett not only wanted to help celebrate that momentous occasion, but also to do some justice to the thought of John Fisher. Whereas Thomas More's thought never went into eclipse, John Fisher's works gathered dust through much of the eighteenth and nineteenth centuries. In fact, worse was in store for John Fisher's memory. James Anthony Froude, the reigning historian of the English Reformation during Victorian times, blithely spoke of John Fisher as a man "of childish credulity," who "doggedly adhered to his assertions of his own innocence" and thereby "forced himself upon his fate" and whose "babbling tongue would have trumpeted his victory to all the winds."[1]

This shallow perspective on Fisher was to receive its due corrective in the hands of Thomas E. Bridgett, who had not yet thought much of John Fisher when he was an undergraduate at St. John's College, Cambridge, Fisher's own College. Nor was Bridgett yet a Catholic when he was obliged to leave St John's simply because he could not in good conscience take the oath of Royal Supremacy, an oath still required at that time from anyone wishing to take a degree. Bridgett turned to the Catholic Church only after attending the famous lecture-series which Newman gave on "Anglican Difficulties"[2] in the late spring and early summer of

1850. But as a Redemptorist, Bridgett did not turn to writing until the mid-1870s and it was not until 1881 that he brought out his first major historical study, *The History of the Eucharist in Great Britain,* in which several pages foreshadow the overriding interest he was to take in John Fisher during the following years. Partly because of Bridgett's scholarly labors, Fisher was beatified on December 9, 1886, although only two years later did the public at large receive the fruit of those labors, Bridgett's *Life of Blessed John Fisher,* a book republished several times during next three decades.[3] Bridgett's book, which greatly intrigued Gladstone,[4] was bursting with previously unpublished documents and gave precious glimpses of John Fisher, the thinker, and, above all, of his towering moral stature. Bridgett, of course, made ample use of *The English Works of John Fisher,* a volume issued in 1876 by the Early English Texts Society.

That volume could hardly serve as the principal source for shedding light on John Fisher's visceral intellectual engagement in defense of the Faith. For that, one has to turn to Fisher's Latin works, which already in his day had their readability diminished through their length. The relative shortness of the present work was therefore, in all likelihood, one of the reasons why Mgr. Hallett's choice fell on it. But as one most familiar with the thought and times of John Fisher, Mgr. Hallett had a far more important reason for making his choice. The reason related to the subject of the book, the priesthood.

For Fisher the priesthood, which he as a bishop possessed in its fullness, was the summary and nerve center of the Christian dispensation. In line with age-old Catholic tradition, he held that the salvation secured by Christ on the cross was to be imparted to all generations through the sacraments. Among the sacraments the central position has always been assigned to the Eucharist or Mass, whose celebration was the sole privilege of the priesthood. Moreover, Fisher, bishop of Rochester, was a saint. For only a saint could unflinchingly face up over several years to the prospect of ending up on the gallows or on the block. For decades before he was beheaded he lived up, day after day, to the theological norm, according to which, as set forth among others by Thomas Aquinas, no ecclesiastical office demands a higher degree of sanctity than the office of bishop.[5]

As an outstanding scholar of his time, John Fisher could have blamed the small print with which most books were printed at that time (and read at candlelight) for the chronic ailment of his eyes. But Fisher's eyes were even more strained by the fact that he often wept through his celebration of the Mass. He made sure that whenever he celebrated the Mass he would be vividly reminded of its awesome significance. It became true in his case too that saints are apt to make more use of external aids than the very imperfect who would be really in need of such prompting. The King's agents, who drew up an inventory of Fisher's possession following his imprisonment in the Tower, listed among the items in "the broad gallery" of his episcopal residence "a St John's head on the altar."[6] The head in question may have been a painting of a skull, or a real skull, refashioned as the severed head of John the Baptist, Fisher's patron saint. (The significance of this will appear from the very moment, June 1529, when Henry VIII made the first vain move to enlist John Fisher on behalf of his evil scheme to ease his "troubled conscience.") The chief decor of the altar in the great chapel was "a table [painting on a wood panel] of Doomsday." The bishop of Rochester wanted to be reminded in this way too of what alone really counted in human life.

Approaching either one or the other of those altars meant therefore for John Fisher a renewal of the sense of self-immolation, the way most appropriate for priests to unite with Christ as they sacramentally render present on the altar His self-immolation on the cross. It is no idle guess to speculate on John Fisher's feelings as he went in spirit to the Station Church of Saints Cosmas and Damien on the Thursday following the Third Sunday of Lent, and prayed with the words of the "Secret" for that Mass: "We honor the glorious death of your saints, O Lord, in the offering of this sacrifice from which all martyrdom takes its origin."[7]

With such a disposition Fisher could feel but profound abhorrence on reading Luther's increasingly violent attacks on the Mass. First came, in 1520, Luther's *De captivitate babylonica ecclesiae. Praeludium*. Possibly at no other time did the word "prelude" encapsulate so well the thrust of a furious symphony to follow. Luther wanted not so much a reform of the abuses in the administration and reception of the sacraments. He aimed at a radical rewriting of Christian faith and with a logic that could only lead to an essential disregard of the sacraments. The very start of Luther's book was more than enough to justify the sounding of the alarm throughout Christendom: "To begin with I must deny that there are seven sacraments, and for the present maintain that there are but three: baptism, penance and the bread. All three have been subjected to a miserable captivity by the Roman curia, and the church has been robbed of all her liberty."[8]

Actually, Luther in his book enslaved those three sacraments as well to his new-fangled principle of justification by faith alone. That principle left no logical room for the sacraments, not even for the one sacrament of baptism, let alone for three and much less for all the seven sacraments, including that of the priesthood. It was another matter that an already fifteen-centuries-long Christian tradition made it impossible to implement right away that logic in its full rigor, although some momentous efforts were made. It was still another matter that desperate attempts were made by some post-Luther Protestants to justify their practice of baptizing (especially of children), breaking the bread, and having "ordained" ministers. Today's ecumenical climate often prevents the perception of the logic that what was emphatically denied (and lost, or rather thrown away) five hundred years ago, cannot be recovered by wishful thinking, however well-intentioned and dressed in distinctions that amount to theological hairsplitting.

In England, where the infiltration of Luther's ideas had been watched with growing concern ever since he nailed his 95 theses on the door of the Castle Church of Wittenberg on October 31, 1517, the need was felt for momentous action, once he came out

INTRODUCTION   XI

with this *Babylonian Captivity*. The action took place on May 12, 1521, the octave of the Ascension, at St. Paul's Cross, where well over ten thousand[9] Londoners gathered to watch the burning of the works of Luther, Carlstadt and others, and to hear a sermon by John Fisher, the most learned ecclesiastic then in England. By then Fisher had been chancellor of Cambridge University for fifteen years as well as bishop of Rochester. By then all of learned Europe had been familiar with Erasmus' repeated encomium of Fisher as "the one man at this time who is incomparable for uprightness of life, for learning and for greatness of soul."[10]

Fisher preached at the request of Cardinal Wolsey, Archbishop of York and the Pope's *legatus a latere*. On Fisher's right were seated the Pope's ambassador and William Warham, Archbishop of Canterbury, on his left the imperial ambassador and the bishop of Durham, with the rest of the bishops seated around. Of course, only a part of the crowd could hear the words of Fisher and very few must have been those who could keep their attention alive through the two hours which it took for Fisher to deliver his sermon, which was promptly published.[11] During the sermon Cardinal Wolsey kept in his hands a copy of the King's *Assertio septem sacramentorum*,[12] a memorable royal reply to Luther's *De captivitate babylonica*. The King himself was so pleased with Fisher's sermon, that he ordered its being translated into Latin so that all Christendom might benefit. There is therefore ample reason to include it in modern English as an Appendix in this volume.

The King came to regret his action. Years later he commanded the destruction of all copies of Fisher's sermon. No wonder. Luther's attack on the sacraments in the *Babylonian captivity* made no sense unless the very hierarchical structure of the Church was dismissed. This is why Fisher emphasized so much in his sermon against Luther the mission and authority of the pope and bishops as something ordained by Christ himself.

Emphasis on that authority is equally present in Fisher's *Defence of the Priesthood,* or Fisher's reply to Luther's *De abroganda missa privata Martini Lutheri sententia*.[13] The latter, published in

1522, contained sallies such as that the Mass was "surely the devil's work," "a disgrace and dishonor to the holy testament of Christ," that "nothing in this world should be so studiously avoided and despised as these fine-appearing spiritual counterfeits, masses, services, faith, and clergy," and that "it would be better to be a devil and a murderer than a priest or a monk" who still continued celebrating the Mass.[14] Luther offered infinitely more than just his opinion (sentence) on the Mass. In order to plead that the Mass be abrogated he had to pass a death-sentence upon it.

Fisher began his reply, *Sacri sacerdotii defensio* ("The Defence of the Holy Priesthood"), by reminding his readers of Luther's call to a violent crusade against Mass and priests. Fisher, of course, could have filled not one but a dozen pages with Luther's invectives against Mass, priests, bishops and pope. Fisher was fully entitled to write that all those invectives fit "no one else so exactly" as Luther himself: "An impudent mouth, blasphemous cheeks, the belching of ungovernable pride, a tongue inflamed by Satan against Christ speaking through Saint Paul, the vomiting of mad words, . . . an ambition greater than Lucifer's." In sum Luther was "a veritable Behemoth . . . covered by the impenetrable scales of deceit."[15] These dozen or so lines, filled with expressions taken from Luther's works that were bursting with them, were Fisher's sole protracted descent into the lower levels of controversial theologizing. Throughout *The Defence* Fisher kept to arguments and reasoning, free of invective, qualifying only now and then Luther's attacks as curses, which in fact were formulated by Luther exactly as curses. Fisher argued, or rather enunciated the Catholic truth and supported it with arguments. He did not engage in disputation. For as Fisher stated in his best anti-Lutheran book, *Contra Oecolampadium*, Saint Paul "does not say, reject a heretic after the first and second disputation, but after the first and second admonition. When that has been made to no effect, he is an acknowledged enemy, and we must repel his attack as we choose, not as he chooses."[16]

Fisher's line of argument kept its momentous relevance. It is a precious evidence among many that the age-old doctrine about the Mass was not deformed by abuses of the celebration of the Mass during the decades immediately preceding Luther's rise. Fisher's book is a powerful rebuttal of Luther's claim that the doctrine about the Mass had to be restored to its pristine form. Fisher's book is one more rebuttal of those today who try to justify Luther on precisely that score. Fisher's book has a momentous relevance for today when Luther's and his successors' teaching about the Eucharistic rite is set up as something the Catholic Church has to accommodate in one way or another. Fisher's book fully justified, decades in advance, the anathemas which the Council of Trent was to hurl at Luther's teaching.

Fisher wrote a century or so before Galileo's telescope demolished once and for all the ancient teaching about the superior material quality of the heavenly regions. Therefore he was allowed to argue briefly, on two occasions, that nature itself shows a hierarchical arrangement which is fully found in the Church. More than balancing this dated detail is the stab at feminism which lurks in Fisher's rebuttal of Luther's advocacy of universal priesthood and of his trying to get around Saint Paul's ruling that women should not raise their voice in the Church. "See, dear reader," Fisher introduces his unveiling of what is implied in Luther's position, "how Luther conjures up his female priests from nowhere." And he concludes: "But Luther wishes to curry favour with the ladies."[17] Such remarks should seem to have a prophetic ring today when most Lutheran Synods, and in general most Protestant churches that still keep some semblance of priesthood, yield rather easily to the pressures of feminism.

Fisher's warning on woman priests should have a special relevance for his own England where the Established Church went ahead with the ordination of women and thereby deprived itself of the last semblance of its desire to be known as part of the Catholic Church. It is the last phase of the process whereby Lutheran theologians began to sap, during the reign of Edward VI

(1547–1553), genuine Catholic ingredients in the Church of England. Its founder, Henry VIII, who to his dying days desperately clung to the Catholic notion of the Mass (and thereby of the priesthood), would be gasping for words if he could see the Church of England making a mockery of the sacrament of the priesthood by ordaining women, while other Episcopalians (with far less interest in Catholicism) have now even women bishops. And if Henry VIII were to wonder why only the Church of Rome holds out against the juggernaut of feminism, he might even spot the reason in that highest form of firmness available to Rome alone, which is an infallible papal utterance.

Such an utterance was the Apostolic Letter issued by John Paul II in late May 1994. There the pope referred to the "living Magisterium" as knowing of no authorization that could justify the ordination of women. That the Apostolic Letter had an infallible character should have been clear right there and then to anyone except to the deliberately myopic. At any rate, that character has been reaffirmed by Rome in late 1995. Shortly before that, Rome also had to acknowledge, in a roundabout way, that its ecumenical strategy toward Protestants had to be scrapped for all practical purposes. The centerpiece of that strategy was the Church of England as a bridgehead towards other Protestant Churches. For whatever the patently Protestant character of the 39 Articles, the Anglican rituals (as articulated in its Prayerbook) have some Catholic thrust. By proceeding with the ordination of women, the Church of England burnt up a crucially needed bridge for its approaches to Rome. The bridge related to the rite of the Eucharist, the very center of all Christian rites and inseparable from the priesthood. It may also be noted, that sometime before the ordination of women came to a head within the Church of England, its theologians in the Anglican Roman Catholic Interfaith Commission (ARCIC) failed, not without the baffling connivance of their Catholic counterparts, to provide meaningful assurance about the Catholic character of its doctrine of the priesthood.

It should seem telling that in his *Defence of the Priesthood* Fisher does not think it important to dwell on any pretended abuse about the Mass. In fact, Luther himself made it absolutely clear[18] that he wanted to abolish the Mass as a sacrifice and not simply prune it from abuses. For Luther considered the Mass, as taken for a true sacrifice within the Catholic tradition, to be the invention of the devil. Luther fully knew that his doctrine of justification by faith alone was incompatible with sacramental priesthood, in fact with the administration of any sacrament. Thus it became his problem why the sacrament of baptism, and especially infant baptism, was still to be administered as necessary for salvation. This and other problems inherent in Luther's position did not go away just because Melanchthon almost succeeded in glossing over the clarity of his master's doctrine.

In *The Defence* Fisher comes back again and again to the all-important point that if the Catholic doctrine of the sacrifice of the Mass and priesthood was erroneous, then the Church must have been teaching a grave error from almost the very start. For whatever one's interpretation of the New Testament, the Church Fathers have been unanimous in holding the Catholic teaching on the Eucharist as a sacrifice that can be offered only by a specially ordained priesthood acting in the role of Christ.

Fisher's argument was not new at all, and certainly not in his beloved England where a Wycliff and others had already spread abroad doctrines that anticipated Luther. Thomas Netter of Walden, Provincial of the English Carmelites, already in the early fifteenth century warned against those who denied the essential unity of the sacrifice of Christ on Calvary and the Eucharist: "There are not many Christs, the doctors explain, but one Christ is offered in every place, and we do not perform another sacrifice but always the same; not merely of the same general class or of the same kind . . . but the same in its essence and in what it consists, truly and numerically one. It is this that is the one sacrifice of Christians. Whoever would deny this oneness contradicts the Apostle."[19]

Fisher was still to be restored to fame when in 1857 the Anglican Bishop Alexander Forbes of Brechin (Scotland) issued a pastoral letter in which he argued that unless the sacrifice of the Eucharist is held to be one, in some mysterious way, with the sacrifice of the Cross, one cannot escape the inference that the Church "has erred from the beginning." For according to the Bishop "the ancient doctors teach that the Eucharistic Sacrifice is the same substantially with that of the Cross."[20] For holding this view on the strict unity of the two sacrifices, Bishop Forbes was, two years later, arraigned before his fellow Anglican bishops and ultimately censured by them.

A telling feature still to be noted about Fisher's *Defence of the Priesthood* is that he quotes there five times Eusebius' *Church History*. Eusebius' work, that had been printed at least a dozen times by 1521, is a storehouse of exclusive information about the first three centuries of the Church. Much of what is extant, for instance, from the writings of Saint Dionysius, bishop of Alexandria during Decius and Valerian, is known today because Eusebius quotes him at length. In fact, no pre-Nicene Father is quoted by Eusebius at such length as bishop Dionysius. Thus it may be fairly assumed that Fisher was fully familiar with bishop Dionysius' view that to avoid any act whereby the unity of the Church would be severed was even more meritorious than to refuse sacrificing to the idols.

In writing to Novatian, who as a presbyter of Rome set himself up against the bishop of Rome, Dionysius warns him: "You ought to have been ready to suffer anything rather than split the Church of God, and martyrdom to avoid schism would have brought you as much honour as martyrdom to escape idolatry—I should say, more. For in the latter case a man is martyred to save his own single soul, in the former to save the whole Church."[21] In saying this Dionysius voiced a general consensus about the evil of schism and anticipated the pithy phrase which Augustine flung in the face of the Donatist bishop, Parmenian: "Schism is the most sacrilegious of all sins, because there can be no just cause whatever for rending the unity of the Church."²²

In Dionysius' letter Fisher could not only see anticipated his own tying of the priesthood to loyalty to Rome, but would also find spiritual comfort for his failure to keep Henry VIII loyal to the tenets which the King articulated in his *Assertio septem sacramentorum* against Luther. "Even now," Dionysius continues his pleading with Novatian, "if you were to persuade or coerce your fellow-Christians into unanimity, your fall would count for less than your recovery [from drifting into schism]—the first will be forgotten, the second applauded. If they will not listen, and there is nothing you can do, by all means save your soul."²³

Fisher succeeded in persuading only Thomas More about the strict primacy of the bishop of Rome as the pledge of the unity of all Christians.²⁴ This, in view of Thomas More's saintly probity, tells much about the limit of the power of persuasion by arguments. It seems that for Thomas More a chief reason for taking to heart the arguments of the bishop of Rochester was the latter's indubitable personal holiness.

Fisher's *Defense of the Priesthood* appeared in 1525, simultaneously with his refutation of Luther's attacks on Henry VIII's *Assertio*. A mere two years later the admiration of the King for Fisher began to sour and during the following seven years turned into a hatred that could be satisfied only by the taking of Fisher's life. The story of those nine years has been often told and in great detail, but an aspect of it has failed to be given proper focus. For no sooner had the King's "troubled conscience" begun to be discussed in a formal way than Fisher found himself almost alone in his refusal to see merit in the King's cause, a refusal that prompted telling reactions. The first of these instances came when in the secret court, attended by the King himself in June 1527, Fisher roundly took exception to Archbishop Warham's statement that all the bishops present had put their seal and signature on the document that demanded a ruling from Campeggio, the papal legate, on the validity of Henry's marriage with Catherine of

Aragon. At first, the King voiced his disbelief at Fisher's disclaimer. Then, after Fisher made it clear to Warham that he [Warham] had put his [Fisher's] seal on the document without his consent, the King tried to make Fisher's dissent appear to be of no consequence. He did this with the contemptuous remark addressed to Fisher: "Well, well, it shall make no matter, we will not stand with you in argument herein, for you are but one man."[25] But it quickly dawned on the Court that Fisher was truly a man the very same way that John the Baptist was a man.

For even then Fisher implied that the King's case was based on "feigned occasion," that is, on a spurious ground that distorted the real issue. According to Fisher the real issue was not whether the Bull of dispensation of Pope Julius II, whereby Henry was free to marry Catherine, the widow of his brother, had legal blemishes or not, but whether the pope did grant the dispensation. Since he did, Henry's marriage with Catherine was valid and therefore could not be dissolved by any power, divine or human. But Fisher said more than that when, to the surprise of the Legatine Court, he delivered a long speech, on behalf of Catherine at its fifth session, July 28, 1529. The substance of the speech survived through the pen of Campeggio's secretary.

Fisher first referred to his "two years of diligent study,"[26] the results of which he had to make manifest or else he would be failing in his duty. Then Fisher spoke of the possible damnation of his soul (the table of Doomsday on the altar in his large chapel was clearly in his mind) were he not to serve the truth. This forced him "to declare, to affirm, and with forcible reasons to demonstrate to them [members of the Court] that this marriage of the king and the queen can be dissolved by no power, human or divine, and for this opinion he declared he would even lay down his life." Then he referred to the example of John the Baptist and to the fact that since Christ's sacrifice the bond of marriage had greatly increased in holiness: "The Baptist in olden times regarded it as impossible for him to die more gloriously than in the cause of marriage, and that as it was not so holy at that time as it has now become by the shedding of Christ's blood." In this he found so much encouragement as "to dare any great or extreme peril whatever." Then after adding "many other suitable words," he handed over to the Legate a handwritten booklet containing his reasoning on the subject. Then the secretary noted that Fisher's intervention created a stir, leaving everyone wondering: "What he will do we shall know when the day comes. You already know what sort of a man he is, and may imagine what is likely to happen."[27] Prophetic words indeed and a most accurate characterization of the kind of man Fisher was. His fellow bishops on the Court were men of very different texture. They reproached him for prejudging the case.

A part of Fisher's booklet survived. It shows him at his reasoning best. As in his *Defence of the Priesthood* he begins with listing his axioms, all of which go the heart of the matter and must have greatly inconvenienced those ready to hide behind the facade of legal niceties. The King, obviously trying to seek refuge in legal obfuscation, was enraged and ordered Stephen Gardiner, a young Cambridge divine, to write a reply. The latter is of interest only because of the reference there to Fisher's own reference to John the Baptist. Gardiner's comment was: "O voice devoid of all modesty and gravity!" To which Fisher added a marginal note in his copy of Gardiner's reply: "What more did I attest than the cardinal [Wolsey] who [affirmed] that he would be burnt or torn limb from limb rather than act contrary to justice." Fisher was kind enough to refrain from noting that for Wolsey the justice in question was to satisfy the King's contrived conscience.

Fisher, a saint, was humble enough to leave without comment Gardiner's pouncing on his presumed pride: "As if indeed, alone of all men, Rochester was gifted with discernment, and alone had investigated and illuminated the truth of this cause." Gardiner lashed at the injustice of Fisher's seeing his stance as identical with that of John the Baptist. To make the irony complete, Gardiner defended the King from the implication that he was falling into the role of Herod. One can only shudder on

Gardiner's defense of the King as one "always far removed from Herod's cruelty." Then he dared Fisher to come forward and as one upon whom Henry had lavished many favors, "cast Herod's tyranny in our teeth."[28]

A tyrant Henry VIII was. Dickens, no lover of Catholics, has put this way "the plain truth" about Henry: "He was a most intolerable ruffian, a disgrace to human nature, and a blot of blood and grease upon the History of England."[29] It is indeed impossible to put it more concisely. Henry possibly had advance knowledge of two attempts on Fisher's life in 1531, one in the form of poisoned food, another by gunshot. He made himself even more of a marked man when during the few weeks Parliament met in 1529, he resolutely opposed a bill, which he clearly saw to be the fateful first step to deprive the ecclesiastical courts of their independence. Fisher remained undaunted. He preached a great sermon in mid-June on behalf of the validity of Catherine's marriage, an act all the more daring because by then Henry had begun to show off openly Anne Boleyn as his presumed wife and queen. Catherine began to fear for Fisher's life. She begged Fisher not to come to Parliament, but in vain. Chapuys, the ambassador of Emperor Charles, Catherine's nephew, reported to his master: "It is no use, for he is resolved to come and to speak more boldly than he has ever done should he die a hundred thousand times."[30] Meanwhile a third attempt was made on Fisher's life, this time by robbers.

In 1533 matters came to a head. Early that year Henry married Anne Boleyn. On April 6 Fisher was placed under house arrest in charge of Gardiner, Bishop of Winchester. On May 23 Cranmer declared Catherine's marriage invalid. A week later Anne Boleyn was crowned queen in Westminster Abbey. On June 14 Fisher was allowed to return to Rochester, since all of Henry's aims had been achieved, except one. Less than a month later the Pope declared the marriage of Henry and Anne to be invalid. This could only increase Henry's eagerness to get even with Fisher. The pretext for this came when Fisher spoke highly of the holiness of

Elizabeth Barton, who went down in history as "the nun of Kent." She was also believed to have had private revelations. According to one of them Henry VIII would not be king in "seven months" were he to marry Anne Boleyn. The agents of the king began now to seek out all ecclesiastics who had supported the nun in one way or another, to implicate them in high treason. Fisher was to die in a far worthier and portentous matter, one that did full justice to his unbending probity.

No sooner had Parliament met in January 1534 than Fisher was summoned to appear. He begged Cromwell for consideration: "Now almost six weeks I have had a grievous cough with a fever of the beginning thereof, as divers other here in this country hath had, and divers have died thereof, and now the matter is fallen down into my legs and feet with such swelling and ache that I can neither ride nor go." He was sixty-five, an old age when the average life expectancy was below thirty. He pleaded in vain. At the end of February he wrote to the King, but without asking his mercy on the charge that he had connived with the nun in her criticisms of the King. He spoke again of his miserable condition, adding that his "life may not long continue." He begged the King's favor that "he may be delivered of this business, and only to prepare my soul to God and so make it ready against the coming of death, and no more to come abroad in the world."[31] Later he wrote a long letter to the Lords, telling them that he never approved that dire prediction against the King, nor was he consulted by the nun about her revelations. Finally, he begged his fellow Lords to try him not through a royal attainder, used against fugitive criminals, but through the Courts.

During the Spring of 1534 Parliament enacted two momentous laws: one was the Act of Succession which forced the King's subjects to recognize his marriage to Anne Boleyn, and the other, the Act of Royal Supremacy. Before the latter Act was proclaimed on May 1st, Fisher was summoned, on April 13th, to his residence in Lambeth to tender his oath on the former Act. Fisher left Rochester in full awareness he would never return there. It was common knowledge that even if the greatest care had been taken of his health, he would not live for another year. On being shown the text of the oath, Fisher expressed his willingness to recognize Anne Boleyn's child as Henry's legitimate successor, but not the validity of his marriage to Anne. Thomas More took the same position. About this distinction, which was approved by Cranmer, Cromwell quickly perceived that it would be equivalent to recognizing the pope's authority in the matter of Henry's attempted marriage with Anne. With the Act of Royal Supremacy ready to be proclaimed such a distinction would have been its refutation. About the same time, April 14, the Nun of Kent and four priests were hanged and quartered at Tyburn.

In early May Queen Catherine refused the oath of succession. She was immediately removed to Kimbolton where she lingered in great seclusion until she died in early January 1536. In mid-May of 1535 both Fisher and More were confined to the Tower. Before then, on January 15, 1535, the King had been declared "the supreme head on earth of the English Church."[32] Meanwhile Parliament came up with a stricter version of the Act of Succession, which, if retroactive, could have legalized the imprisonment of Fisher and More. Then the Parliament enacted what became known as the Third Act. It enlarged on the 1532 statute of Treason, making it high treason to oppose the King or the Queen in any way whatsoever. Therefore the mere refusal to take the oath on the Acts of Succession and of Royal Supremacy could be construed as a direct rebellion against the Sovereign. Thence Fisher, More and countless others could be sentenced to death without further ado.

Two bishops who attempted to sway Fisher while in the Tower recalled their cowardly behavior with deep remorse in subsequent years. One of them, Bishop Stokesley of London, would say in tears: "O that I had holden still with my brother Fisher and not left him when time was!"[33] Then six or seven of his fellow bishops came as a group to plead with him. His answer to them could be seen as an elaboration on Jesus's words to the women who lamented over Him as he approached Calvary. He reminded them that it would have been their common duty "to stick together in repressing these violent and unlawful intrusions and injuries, daily offered to our common mother and holy Church of Christ rather than by any manner of persuasion to help or set forward the same." And as if to throw the gauntlet at Henry and his band, in the name of the supremacy of the spiritual as established by Christ, he told the bishops: "We ought rather to seek by all means the temporal destruction of these ravening wolves that daily go about worrying and devouring everlastingly the flock that Christ hath committed to our charge, than to suffer them thus to range abroad." Here spoke the priest, who lived up fully to his defence of the awesome dignity and responsibility of the priesthood. He could only bemoan that many priests and bishop failed to do so: "The fort is betrayed even of them that should have defended it. And therefore, seeing the matter thus begun and so faintly resisted on our parts, I fear we be not the men that shall see the end of the misery." Though he was alone a man among them, he humbly spoke as if he had been one of those who failed to act as befitted men.

A true priest had also to be perspicacious. Very instructive in this respect is Fisher's gentle rebuttal of Richard Wilson, his attendant in the Tower, a man as simple as he was good, who told him that the King would expect not a whit more from Fisher than just to hear from his lips the words that he was the Head of the Church. Fisher replied: "Tush, tush, thou art but a fool and knowest little what this matter meaneth, but hereafter thou mayest know more. But I tell thee it is not for the supremacy only that I am thus tossed and troubled, but also for an oath [succession] which if I would have sworn, I doubt whether I should have ever been questioned for the supremacy or no." Indeed the Act of Succession implied the rejection of papal supremacy, an act utterly incompatible with the notion of Catholic priesthood as Fisher expounded it in its defence.

Shortly before Christmas 1534 he appealed to the King, through Cromwell, for some alleviation of his miseries "in this cold and painful imprisonment." It is not known whether his request was granted, but he was allowed ink and pen. Apart from that, he had to pay 15 shillings (a large sum then) every week for his sustenance and his servant's in the Tower. He used his pen and ink to write two short meditations to his half-sister, Elizabeth White, a Dominican nun, whom Queen Catherine held dear, partly because she so much resembled her brother. The two meditations are known as *A Spiritual Consolation* and *The Ways to Perfect Religion*. Fisher's modern biographer, E. E. Reynolds' remarks about the latter work that its theme was the Four Last Things—death, judgment, heaven, and hell, and that "the reader of today may be repelled by the preacher's [Fisher's] stern condemnation of sin and by repeated warnings of the wrath to come."[34]

Yet the reader of today would not be able to grasp much of Fisher's animated defence of the priesthood, if he or she had not been possessed of a vivid realization of the seriousness of sin. For if the last thirty years have shown anything it is the fact that in the measure in which the seriousness of sin is underplayed in catechetical instruction and in theological treatises, realization of what is meant by death, judgment, heaven and hell also peters out. As a consequence one feels less the need of a priesthood properly so-called. But in speaking of priests, Fisher did not speak of glorified psychological counselors but of indispensable instruments of eternal salvation.

It was in view of that salvation that he marched willingly toward the block on Tower Hill, across the moat of the fortress itself, in the morning of June 22, to be beheaded. His last comfort was to chance in the New Testament he carried with him on the words: "This is life everlasting that they may know thee, the only true God, and Jesus Christ whom thou has sent. I have glorified thee upon the earth. I have finished the work that thou gavest me to do" (John 17:3-4). It was most fitting that the one who labored so much to prevent Luther from appropriating to himself the Gospel and depriving thereby the faithful from its truly Catholic meaning should be strengthened by Gospel in the final moments of his great trial. He also must have known that the next day was the vigil of the Feast of the birth of John the Baptist. Within a few minutes Fisher was born into eternal companionship with the Saint whose example and intercession proved to be for him such a firm guidance and unfailing source of strength that he fully exemplified what it is to be a priest.

It was not out of pity that the King changed, in apparently the last minute, the manner of Fisher's execution from hanging and disemboweling to beheading. He may have remembered his jest, uttered when he first heard, towards the end of May, that Fisher had been created a cardinal: "Well, let the pope send him a hat, when he will; but I will so provide that whensoever it cometh, he shall wear it on his shoulders, for head he shall have none to set it on."[35] Henry must have felt that by implementing this jest of his, he would make more effective his campaign, which he began a few weeks before the beheading, to vilify Fisher's reputation in England as well as abroad. He also must have realized that a mere beheading would create less revulsion, at least in foreign parts, than the other way of execution.

Still, Henry did his best to show the extent of his fury by ordering that Fisher's headless body should lie naked on the scaffold for the rest of the day. Armed guards saw to it that no one treat the body with any form of respect. In the evening the body was laid to rest with great haste in the churchyard of All Hallows, at a stone's throw from the scaffold. It was there that the headless body of Thomas More was also laid to rest. When More's daughter obtained permission to rebury her father in the little church St. Peter ad Vincula within the Tower compounds, Fisher's body too seems to have been transferred there.

When the Muslims overran Hippo, Catholics ransomed the body of St. Augustine by paying its weight in gold. Catholics all over the world would, no doubt, readily collect twice as much gold as Fisher's bones may still weigh and rebury them in a Catholic sanctuary. It is, however, most doubtful that the Established Church would be ready for a bargain which the Muslims did not refuse. A few years ago some Catholics began to have a Mass said in the dungeon where John Fisher spent his last months. Encouraged, they asked permission for an annual Mass to be said in St. Peter ad Vincula. On being told that only the Queen, the Head of the Church of England, could grant the permission, they applied, but in vain. They were told, through the Lord Chancellor, that they can hold there any devotion, but no Mass. Fisher's defence of the priesthood and of the Eucharist, as properly understood, casts indeed a very long shadow. Fisher certainly understood—and the heirs of his erstwhile antagonists understand it all too well in their own way—that the Mass, as celebrated by the priest, remains the very center of Faith as universally understood until Luther claimed to have discovered the "biblical truth" about it.

Those heirs are miscalculating no less than Henry miscalculated. The end of the papacy, which the ageing Luther predicted to come within a few decades, is far from being in sight four and a half centuries later. But increasingly visible is the handwriting on the walls of the Establishment that Newman called a "mimic Catholicism" and a "wreck".[36] Today he would denounce it explicitly as a "moral wreck."[37] It truly lives up to the pattern set by its Founder, who from defending the faith went on to defend rank immorality.

Henry failed to perceive that it would have been to his great advantage to let Fisher die quietly in prison or even in house arrest; his death was expected to come perhaps within a few months. Nor did Henry reckon with the fact that Fisher's parboiled head was the head of a saint. Stuck on a pole on London Bridge it did not begin to shrivel and to frighten. Within a week or two it became known even in Germany that Fisher's head "grew more florid and life-like, so that many expected it would speak—a thing we read in the acts of certain martyrs."[38]

A martyr he was and not one of Froude's and other gurus' garrulous, babbling, old men who, according to an ancient English proverb, "tell no tales" once they have died. It is as a martyr that Fisher, though dead, still speaks: *defunctus adhuc loquitur.* He indeed speaks most eloquently through his *Defence of the Priesthood*, a title which, if fully faithful to the original title set by Fisher, should rather read: "Defence of the *Holy* Priesthood."

The Feast of the Assumption, 1996   S. L. J.

[1] A. Froude, *History of England from the Fall of Wolsey to the Death of Elizabeth* (New York: Charles Scribner, 1871), vol. II, pp. 208-29. In fairness to Froude it should be pointed out that the context of these disparaging remarks of his is his portrayal of Fisher's role in the affair of the Nun of Kent, to be discussed later. But even in context where it was simply impossible to ignore Fisher's virtues, Froude offsets his grudging acknowledgment of them with phrases, such as that Fisher was "weak, superstitious, pedantical" (p. 284) and in facing up to Fisher's martyrdom, he emphasizes more its tragic features than its witness to Fisher's heroism (pp. 336-37). This is not the place to take issue with Froude's principal contention, namely, that had Henry VIII not stood up to Rome, England would have become a fiefdom, similar to the Low Countries, of the Spanish.

[2] Republished, with my introduction, in the Real View Books series (Fraser, Mich.: American Council on Economics and Society, 1994).

[3] I am using the 1922 reprinting (London: Burns, Oates & Washbourne). Even more popular was Bridgett's *Life and Writings of Sir Thomas More* (London: Burns and Oates, 1891).

[4] See C. Ryder, *Life of Thomas Edward Bridgett* (London: Burns and Oates, 1906), pp. 155-56.

[5] See *Summa theologiae,* II-II, qu. 135, art. 1.

[6] E. E. Reynolds, *Saint John Fisher* (New York: P. J. Kenedy & Sons, 1955), p. 227.

[7] Or in Latin, "*de quo martyrium sumit omne exordium.*"

[8] Quoted from the English translation, *The Babylonian Captivity of the Church,* in *Luther's Works* (Philadelphia: Muhlenberg Press, 1959), vol. 36, p. 18.

⁹ A foreign observer obviously exaggerated in estimating the crowd at 30,000, a full half of London's population.
¹⁰ See Reynolds, *Saint John Fisher,* p. 42.
¹¹ *The sermon of Iohan the bysshop of Rochester made agayn the pernicyous doctryn of Martin luuther* . . . , as reads the title of the original.
¹² See note 2 to the Appendix.
¹³ For its English translation, with the rather misleading title, *The Misuse of the Mass,* instead of "The Suppression of the Mass," see *Luther's Works,* Volume 36. *Word and Sacrament, II* (Philadelphia: Muhlenberg Press, 1959), pp. 127-230.
¹⁴ See English translation in *Luther's Works,* vol. 36, p. 154. Fisher quotes only some of these invectives.
¹⁵ Ibid., p. 124.
¹⁶ Quoted in Bridgett, p. 116. In the same context Fisher also refers to the methods of Jerome, Augustine and Hilary in dealing with heretics. One does not find them to proceed "with soft and gentle words, but with firm and harsh words, as befits the dedicated defenders of Christ's religion and the enemies of truth and adversaries of faith."
¹⁷ *Defence,* pp. 131-32.
¹⁸ See on this note 8 above.
¹⁹ Netter refers to chapter 10 of the Letter to the Hebrews. Quoted from F. Clark, *Eucharistic Sacrifice and the Reformation* (London: Darton Longman and Todd, 1960), pp. 526.
²⁰ Quoted ibid., p. 248
²¹ *Eusebius. The History of the Church,* tr. G. A. Williamson (Penguin Books, 1965), p. 285.
²² *Contra epistolam Parmeniani* 2:11 (Migne PL, vol. 43, col. 69).
²³ *Eusebius. The History of the Church,* p. 285.
²⁴ See E. E. Reynolds, *St. Thomas More* (Garden City, N.Y.: Doubleday Image Books, 1958), p. 125.
²⁵ For a full transcription of the records, see Reynolds, *Saint John Fisher,* pp. 150-58.
²⁶ The result of that study became the substance of the long essay which Nicholas Harpsfield, the last Catholic archdeacon of Canterbury, collated in part from Fisher's manuscripts. It was first published in W. Eyston's transcription in 1707. A critical edition, *A Treatise on the Pretended Divorce between Henry VIII and Catharine of Aragon,* was the work of Nicholas

Pocock (Oxford: Printed for the Camden Society, 1878), a quarto volume of over 300 pages.
[27] Quoted in Reynolds, *Saint John Fisher*, p. 153.
[28] Ibid., p. 160.
[29] Ch. Dickens, *A Child's History of England* (London: Chapman & Hall, 1906), p. 210.
[30] Reynolds, *Saint John Fisher*, p. 182.
[31] Ibid., p. 204.
[32] *"In Terra Supremum Caput Anglicanae Ecclesiae."* Ibid., p. 239.
[33] Ibid., p. 241.
[34] Ibid., p. 254.
[35] See Bridgett, *Life of Blessed John Fisher*, p. 359.
[36] J. H. Newman, *Anglican Difficulties,* pp. 2-3. See note 2 above. Significantly, Newman made these harsh strictures right at the outset of those much ignored lectures of his. When it came to truth, he did not mince words.
[37] At a time when Dr. Runcie, the former Archbishop of Canterbury, admits on the BBC that he had knowingly ordained practicing homosexuals. In the same context he deplored his Church's reluctance to approve of homosexuality in an unambiguous way. Since the Lambeth conference of 1930 signalled, he argued, that "sexual activity was a blessing even if divorced [by contraceptives] from procreation," it was not logical to frown on "people who engaged in same-sex expression and who are incapable of heterosexual expression" (*The Daily Telegraph*, May 16, 1996). A month or so later, Dr. Carey, the present Archbishop, called for a moral renewal of society, while skirting around the issue whether there are absolutely binding moral commandments. His evasiveness was noted even by the press favorable to the Established Church.
[38] Part of the report by Campeggio's secretary about Fisher's death. Quoted ibid., p. 404.

TRANSLATOR'S PREFACE

THE first edition of Luther's work, *On the Abrogation of the Mass*, was composed towards the end of 1521 and printed in January, 1522. A few months later—it is dated July 15, 1522—he published his reply to the *Assertion of the Seven Sacraments*, the book which gained for Henry VIII the title of 'Defender of the Faith.' So gross and ribald was this reply that Henry considered it beneath his dignity to answer, but both Sir Thomas More and the Bishop of Rochester composed books in defence of their king and the orthodox doctrine of which he was the champion. More's book was published in 1523 under the pseudonym of 'William Ross,' and made Luther, as Stapleton puts it, 'as dumb as a fish.' Fisher held up his book upon reports of Luther's amendment, and meanwhile composed a reply to Luther's book on the Mass— the book which is here presented in English dress. Eventually they were both issued simultaneously in 1525, the one under the title *A Defence of the Assertions of the King of England against Luther's Babylonian Captivity*, the other under the title *Defence of the Sacred Priesthood against Luther*. They were published in Cologne by Quentel, and the latter work was issued in two forms, quarto and duodecimo.

Owing to the circumstances of their composition

the two books mutually refer to each other. In the book in defence of the king, the Bishop of Rochester speaks in one place of the book on the priesthood as already written, in another as to be written; while in the latter work he twice refers to his apology for the king as already written.

The arguments of *The Defence of the Priesthood* are derived from the Holy Scriptures and from the Fathers, in addition to whom the Bishop quotes in one place a number of Jewish Rabbis, in another the decrees of a number of early popes. Sometimes he argues from reason and the nature of the case, but always quoting Scriptural texts in support. His proof from Scripture is cogent and indeed overwhelming, but the quotations from earlier writers must be accepted with caution on account of the uncritical spirit of the time. As against Luther, however, this is not very important, for, though the texts quoted by the holy bishop may have been written some centuries later than he thought, they were and are, nevertheless, witnesses to Catholic tradition, the whole of which, whether early or late, was contemptuously rejected by Luther.

It should be remembered that the book was written before the Council of Trent had imposed upon the Church the use of the Vulgate. Consequently the holy bishop's texts do not always verbally conform to it, though there is rarely any difference in meaning. Sometimes he uses the version which Erasmus had prepared from the Greek and issued as the 'Novum Instrumentum' in 1516. As a rule it has been possible to employ the English translation commonly in use, but any

TRANSLATOR'S PREFACE

important variation has been pointed out in the notes.

As to the quotations from the Fathers and other writers, though the bishop rarely gives definite references we have been able to trace nearly all the passages. Unless otherwise stated, the references are to Migne.[1]

The style of the work is plain and simple. The writer's one object is to be clear and convincing, nor does he ever strive after rhetorical effects. He is, however, frequently moved to anger by Luther's foul blasphemies, and in the passage upon our Lady (p. 130) the tenderness of his devotion is at once obvious. So anxious is he that the strength of his case should not be forgotten that he often repeats his points, and sometimes there is much redundance of language. But although we have occasionally omitted a few words that were purely repetitive we have not thought it consistent with the office of a translator to present the author other than he is. After all, the holy martyr had not the style of a Tacitus or a Tertullian.

It will be well to say a word about the ambiguous term 'presbyteri.' Where it is employed in close connection with 'sacerdotes' we have rendered the one term 'presbyters' or 'elders,' the other 'priests.' Where, however, there could be no possible ambiguity or controversy we have not hesitated to translate 'presbyteri' by its derivative 'priests.'

To select the best method of dividing the text has not been easy. The bishop speaks of his three

---

[1] We owe half-a-dozen of these references to Schmeink's edition of Fisher's work (Münster in Westfalen, 1925).

TRANSLATOR'S PREFACE

rejoinders to Luther's three attacks, but they do not correspond each to each, as will be evident from the page of contents. We have thought it best to divide the book into twenty-five sections in order to facilitate reference to the notes.

As we write these words we are looking forward with hope to the canonization of Blessed John Fisher, together with his friend and companion Blessed Thomas More. The proceeds of the sale of this book will be devoted to the expenses of their cause.

PHILIP E. HALLETT.

Feast of St. Thomas of Canterbury, 1934.

The Defence of the Priesthood

Section 1

PROLOGUE

In which the author explains his intention, his subject-matter, the division and arrangement of the book.

THERE have been published to the world from Luther's printing press many books which I have perused with great grief, for I found scattered throughout them so much of that poison by which innumerable simple souls, day by day, are destroyed. Yet of all that I have seen none is more pestilential, senseless or shameless than the one he entitles *The Abrogation of the Mass*, for in it he tries utterly to destroy the sacrifice of the body and blood of Christ, which the Church has ever held to be most salutary, and the chief object of devotion to all the faithful of Christ. To effect his purpose, with much display of words he contends that there is no visible priesthood, and in every possible way he tries to show that the priesthood to which for so many centuries our forefathers have been accustomed was established partly by the lies of men, partly through the inspiration of Satan. This he asserts almost at the opening of his book: 'If you wish to be truly a Christian, be certain, and never allow yourself to be moved from that certainty, that there is in the New Testament no visible and external priesthood save what has been set up by the lies of men and by Satan.'

To put it briefly, Luther makes three attacks against the sacred priesthood. He brings forward three arguments by which, as with three battering-rams, he imagines that he can utterly destroy this Christian truth. For after he has delivered these three attacks upon the priests he adds: 'I am confident that by these three arguments every pious conscience will be persuaded that this priesthood of the Mass and the Papacy is nothing but a work of Satan, and will be sufficiently warned against imagining that by these priests anything pious or good is effected. All will now know that these sacrificial Masses have been proved to be injurious to our Lord's testament and that therefore nothing in the whole world is to be hated and loathed so much as the hypocritical shows of this priesthood, its Masses, its worship, its piety, its religion. It is better to be a public pander or robber than one of these priests.'

My God! How can one be calm when one hears such blasphemous lies uttered against the mysteries of Christ? How can one without resentment listen to such outrageous insults hurled against God's priests? Who can even read such blasphemies without weeping from sheer grief if he still retains in his heart even the smallest spark of Christian piety?

Trusting therefore in the goodness of our Lord we will in our turn try to launch three attacks against Luther by which as with a sponge we hope to wipe away all the filthy and blasphemous things that have proceeded from his mouth against priests. But, to avoid confusion, lest the reader, when he hears of attacks, should be uncertain whether we mean our own or Luther's, we shall call our attacks rejoinders. Our first rejoinder then shall be the prescriptive right of existing truth which, from the founders of the Church through the orthodox Fathers has come down infallibly to us. The second shall be a series of axioms, drawn from the Holy Scriptures and arranged in due order, by which that priesthood, which he calls a visible one, shall be fully established. The third shall be a clear and direct rebuttal of Luther's objections, one by one. But as we do not wish to waste time with many words we shall at once enter upon our subject.

Section 2

FIRST REJOINDER

Following the example of ancient writers, the author builds up an argument against Luther from the right of prescription.

TERTULLIAN was a writer of early date and of learning so remarkable that St. Cyprian never allowed a day to pass without dipping into his works. On the many occasions when he attacked heretics he always urged against them the prescriptive right of long-accepted truth. Not only against Marcion and Hermogenes did he, with most powerful effect, employ this argument, but he wrote a book against heretics in general, entitled *On Prescription*, in which he adduces numerous reasons to prove, in opposition to the heretics, that Catholic truth enjoys a prescriptive right. Now if it were ever suitable to use the argument of prescription against any heretic on behalf of any doctrine, never could it be more justly used than against Luther in defence of the truth of the priesthood. For to this truth all the churches whose foundation can be traced back to the apostles unanimously bear witness. Any one who will take the trouble to peruse the books written in the earliest times of the

Church's history can easily verify this fact, for there is not one of them which does not make mention of priests, as we are about to show. But if now all the churches throughout the world are served by priests, anointed and consecrated, it is clear that they received this rite of the priesthood from the successors of the apostles, these from the apostles themselves, and the apostles from Christ. Let Luther discover, if he can, any church in the whole world, founded by one of the apostles or one of their followers, which does not possess the priesthood. We on our side can point to a church, founded by the apostles, which in the long succession of its bishops, stretching back to the very beginning, has always observed this rite. If then Luther can bring forward nothing similar, it will be obvious to every unprejudiced mind that, in opposition to his falsehood and new-fangled invention, we are in possession of prescriptive right.

But, it will be said, Luther can quote passages from the Scriptures for his opinion. As to that we shall see later on, but meanwhile let us speak of the teachers from whom, in all probability, the churches now spread over the world have received their doctrines. Of more recent writers I shall say nothing, for no one denies that they all attest a priesthood. Passing over then the innumerable authors of a later age, let us begin with St. Augustine and from him go back in order to still earlier writers.

Proof from early writers of the institution and powers of the Priesthood.

St. Augustine not only uses consistently the term priests for presbyters or elders, but he writes:

'When we read that our Lord, a few days after His Resurrection, breathed upon His disciples and said " Receive ye the Holy Ghost," we must understand that He conferred upon them ecclesiastical power. All that Christ hands over to them is the work of the Holy Ghost, and therefore when He teaches them the rule and form of this rite He says " Receive ye the Holy Ghost."[1] And to show that He is laying down a rule for the Church He adds immediately, " Whose sins ye shall retain, they are retained; and whose sins ye shall forgive, they are forgiven them." This breathing conferred upon the apostles a grace which now is given by the imposition of hands to those who are ordained so that they may be held in greater reverence. Thus the apostle says to Timothy, " Neglect not the grace which is in thee, which was given thee by the imposition of the hands of the presbytery."[2] On the one occasion Christ breathed upon them, that the imposition of hands which was to be performed henceforth might be understood to convey the gift of the Holy Ghost. For as at our Lord's baptism there was a visible appearance so that when baptism was afterwards conferred men might not doubt that the Holy Ghost was given to believers, so also in the case we are considering the sign of the breathing was given in the beginning that henceforth when the Church lays on hands it might be believed that the Holy Ghost is infused.'[3]

To this St. Jerome agrees in his epistle to Evagrius,[4] where he teaches that presbyters and bishops are priests. ' I hear,' he says, ' that a certain person has been so mad as to teach that deacons are superior to presbyters, that is to bishops. The apostle clearly teaches that presbyters and bishops are the same, but what possesses him who is ordained to minister to tables and to widows that he should boast himself superior to those who have power to consecrate the body and blood of Christ? Do you ask my authority? Listen to this. " Paul and Timothy, the servants of Jesus Christ, to all the saints in Christ Jesus who are at Philippi, with the bishops and deacons."[5] Here is another example. In the Acts of the Apostles St. Paul speaks to the priests of a certain church, " Take heed to yourselves, and to all the flock, over which the Holy Ghost hath placed you bishops, to rule the Church of God which He hath purchased with His own blood." '[6] In these words although St. Jerome makes no distinction between bishops and presbyters yet he calls them both priests.

St. Ambrose, too, writing upon the Epistle to Timothy, speaks as follows : ' After the bishop the diaconate receives ordination. Why? Because bishops and presbyters share in one order, for each is a priest. The bishop is first; so that every bishop is a presbyter, but not every presbyter is a bishop, but he is bishop who is first among the presbyters. In fine it is clear that Timothy was an ordained presbyter, but because there was no other presbyter superior to him, he was bishop.'[7] St. Ambrose also wrote a special book on the priestly dignity.[8]

St. Hilary also, writing against the Emperor Constantius, makes mention of priests. ' You sought to win by flattery Paulinus, happy to suffer so much, and then you sent him into exile and thus deprived the church of Treves of so holy a priest,

By your edicts you terrorized the faithful. By changing his place of exile you wearied out Paulinus even to death, you drove him out where the Christian name was unknown, lest he should receive food from your granaries or look to have it profaned from the cave of Montanus and Maximilla.⁹ You terrified the pious multitudes of Milan by the fury of your anger. Your tribunes invaded the sanctuary and forcing their way through the populace by every kind of cruelty dragged away the priests from the altar.'¹⁰

Arnobius also, commenting on the 68th Psalm, says: 'Those who like wild beasts lie in ambush in the reeds of the law, that secretly they may injure the congregation of bulls among the kine of the people, are the heretics. For they seek to injure the congregation of the priests who here are to be understood by the term bulls, as being fit for the service of the altar, among the kine, i.e. the dull and ignorant populace.'¹¹

To these may be added St. Cyprian, who writes thus: 'He therefore who does not believe Christ when He bestows the priesthood on men will begin to believe Him when hereafter He will come to vindicate the dignity of the priesthood. Although I know that to some persons all things of this kind seem ridiculous and visionary, yet they will be found true by those who would rather disbelieve the High Priest than believe His priests.'¹²

In addition Tertullian attacks with his wonted irony laymen who considered themselves equal to priests. 'When we in our pride raise ourselves up against the clergy, then we are all one, then we are all priests, because " He hath made us priests to

God and His Father."[13] But when we are challenged to equal the strictness of priestly life, then we lay aside our insignia and profess ourselves lower than they.'[14] Thus we see that a priesthood was in existence even at that early date, and although elsewhere Tertullian asserts that ordained ministers were differentiated from the laity by the authority of the Church, yet he adds that the dignity of ordination is sanctified by God.

So much for Latin writers: let us now hear what Greek writers think of the priesthood. First we may mention St. John Damascene who, in his book on Purgatory, writes as follows: 'Not without reason was it ordained by the Church's wisest disciples, and handed down by tradition, that in the most holy mysteries the priest should pray for the faithful departed.'[15]

Gennadius again, Bishop of Constantinople, in a letter written to all the faithful, commenting on the words of Christ, 'Freely you have received, freely give,'[16] says: 'Clear and obvious is this command. Here there is nothing ambiguous, nothing beyond our grasp, no need of sophistry. "From Me," He says, "you have received the dignity of the priesthood. If you have bought it from Me; if you have paid anything, great or small, for it, then sell it to others."'[17]

Then we have St. Cyril writing on Leviticus in these words: 'The word of God commands priests to be holy, since they approach close to the altar of God, they have to pray for the people and intercede for the sins of men, and have no inheritance in the land, the Lord Himself being their portion.' And a little further on: 'It ordains therefore that those whose portion is the Lord should be sober, abstemious, watchful at all times and especially when they are in attendance at the altar to beg God's mercy and to offer sacrifice in His sight. These commands still retain their force and are to be diligently observed, for the apostle confirms them with laws of the New Testament. Wherefore laying down a rule of life for priests and rulers of priests, he says that they must not be given to much wine, but be sober.'[18]

St. John Chrysostom, writing on the First Epistle to Timothy, says: 'The dignity of doctor and priest is so high and admirable that in order that those worthy of it may be selected, we should endeavour to obtain the approval of God. Thus the choice used to be made, and now also it is so whenever it is made without interference from the passions of men. When we have no regard to worldly or temporal considerations, then we neither desire any man's favour nor fear any man's hatred. For though we have not in us the fulness of the Holy Ghost, yet it is enough if we have a right intention and a single desire that our election may be according to God. Even the apostles when they chose Matthias were not yet filled with the Holy Ghost, but prefacing their business with prayer, they added him to their number. As they acted without regard to human favour or friendship, so must we act. For if we pay no heed to signs that are clear and evident to all, how can we expect God to reveal to us things that are uncertain? "If you have not been faithful," He says, " in that which is little, who will trust you in that which is great and true?"[19] At that time, indeed, when nothing was done in a purely human way, priests were chosen by prophecy. What does that mean? By the Holy Ghost. For it is the office of prophecy not only to foretell the future, but to announce what is present. Thus Saul was found by prophecy when he was hidden at home. Again by prophecy did God truly assist His servants when the Holy Ghost said: " Separate unto Me Paul and Barnabas."[20] So, too, was Timothy chosen. In his case the apostle perhaps numbers several prophecies, one by which he found Timothy, others by which he circumcised and ordained him, in accordance with his words, " Neglect not the grace which is in thee." '[21]

St. Gregory Nazianzen bears similar witness in his metrical address to the bishops: ' O ye priests who offer unbloody sacrifice! O ye glorious shepherds of souls! O privileged ones, to bear in your hands the image of God! O ye who bring together man and man's infinitely exalted God! Ye are the foundation of the world, the light of life, the pillar of the word of truth, priests of everlasting glorious life, Christ-bearers raised to the noblest rank and on high beholding in joy the scenes of glory.'[22]

St. Basil, too, speaks of priests in his book, *On the Institution of Monks*.[23] Asking whether sins should be confessed to all the faithful or to priests alone, he answers that ' it seems necessary to confess sins to the priests, for to them is committed the dispensation of the mysteries.[24] Thus, too, in olden times we find that penitents confessed their sins to the saints. In the Gospel we read that the people confessed their sins to John the Baptist,[25] and in the Acts of the Apostles that those who were baptized confessed to the apostles.'[26]

Eusebius relates that the Apostle John, after the death of the tyrant, returning from Pathmos to Ephesus, was asked to visit the neighbouring Provinces so that he might found churches in places where there were none; and where they existed, that he might appoint to them priests and ministers according as the Holy Spirit in each case directed him.[27]

Times innumerable does the same writer speak of consecrated bishops and priests. Thus he writes :[28] ' When peace was restored to the churches by the death of Maximin, numberless festivities were celebrated by our people, with the greatest joy and exultation. Everywhere the dedications of churches were solemnized. The priests would come together, not even those afar off complaining of the length of the journey, for no distance seemed long to their charity. The people, too, were united together, and as truly being members of the one body of Christ they rejoiced to be bound and joined together, fulfilling the prophetic vision, so mysteriously uttered, " Bone shall come together to bone, and joint to joint."[29] All the members might truly be said to live by one spirit and to have one soul, for there was one faith in all, one and the same God was worshipped by all, and all in union sang hymns to Him. The priestly duties and all offices of religion were carried out with great splendour. Here was the chorus of singers: "young men and maidens, the old with the young praised the name of the Lord."[30] There the ministers in due order and reverent ceremony carried out the sacred mysteries, the body of venerable, white-haired, bishops and priests being conspicuous from afar off. And if anyone, inspired by the grace of God, preached to the people, all observed perfect silence and with upturned countenance and fixed gaze, seemed to await some heavenly message. Admirable was the reverence of the hearers, admirable the discipline of the priests. One spoke after another, and not only " two or three with the rest judging "[31] according to the word of the apostle, but as many as received the word and power of utterance, according to the prayer of Moses : " Oh, that the whole Church of God might prophesy."[32] Jealousy and envy were unknown ; God's gifts were ministered to the people ; each one, as it is written, " for the edification of the Church,"[33] tried to employ his gifts. All these things were done in charity so that they " prevented one another in honour,"[34] and each one considered the other better than himself. For the unlearned reverenced and welcomed those who had wisdom to instruct the people, whilst the wise and learned in their turn honoured those whose pure life and simple sincerity gave assurance that their sacrifices would be acceptable to God ; for to those was committed the office of offering sacrifice whom a homely simplicity of life preserved in purity of heart.'

Then again Origen, in his sixth homily upon Leviticus,[35] writes : ' At the ordination of a priest it is required that the people be present, that all may know for certain that he who in learning, in sanctity, and in every virtue is pre-eminent among the people, should be chosen for the priesthood. The people are to be present that no one may afterwards have any hesitation or regret about the choice. For this is what the apostle prescribes in the ordination of a priest, " he must have a good testimony of them who are without." '[36]

Though the authors we have adduced are many and of great weight, yet we shall have no difficulty in bringing forward authors yet older, either contemporaries of the apostles or so very close to their times that they merit the name of apostolic.

First we may mention St. Hegesippus who in the fourth book of his commentaries, where he deals in full detail with the reasons on which his faith is grounded, says amongst other things that when he came to Rome he found there many bishops from all parts, meeting together for discourse in all charity, and all professing and teaching the same faith. Speaking, too, of the church of the Corinthians, he says: 'The church of the Corinthians persevered in orthodox teaching up to Primus, its bishop, whom I saw on my voyage to Rome. I stayed with him at Corinth for many days, delighting in the purity of his faith. But when I had come to Rome I remained there until Soter succeeded Anicetus and was in turn succeeded by Eleutherius. In all these ordinations and in others which I saw in various cities, everything was observed in accordance with ancient tradition, the words of the prophets and the commands of our Lord.'[37]

More clearly still does St. Ignatius in his Epistle to the Smyrnaeans[38] speak both of the Mass and of priests. 'It is not lawful without the bishop to offer, to immolate sacrifices or to celebrate Masses, but if it seems to him to be according to the will of God, then the sacrifice will be licit and valid.

All that you do in this present time is alterable, for whilst we have time for repentance we may correct ourselves in God. But as time is uncertain, confession must not be delayed. " Behold the man," he saith, " and his works with him,"[39] as it is written. " Honour," he saith, " God and the king, my son."[40] But I say to you, " Honour God indeed as the creator and lord of all things, but the bishop also as the chief of the priests, who bears the image of God, being like unto the Father in authority and like unto Christ in his priesthood. After these, the king, too, must be honoured. For there is none greater than God nor equal to Him, nor in the Church is there any of higher honour than the bishop who exercises the priesthood of God for the salvation of the world, nor in the army is there any like unto the king who meditates peace and good-will to all princes. For he who honours the bishop will be honoured by God, but he who dishonours him will be denied honour by God. For if he who rebels against the king deserves damnation, how will he who does aught without the authority of the bishop escape the vengeance of God? For the priesthood is the noblest of all dignities entrusted to man, and if any one refuses it honour, he refuses honour to God and to our Lord Jesus Christ, who is the first-born of every creature and alone by nature the high-priest of God." '[41]

St. Polycarp, a contemporary of the apostles and a disciple of St. John the apostle, in his Epistle to the Philippians admonishes the people to obey the priests, saying: ' Be ye subject to your presbyters and deacons as to God and Christ.'[42]

Dionysius, in addition to what he says in his *Ecclesiastical Hierarchy*, writes thus to the monk Demophilus :[43] ' Listen now to our judgement. It is unlawful for a priest to be judged by sacred ministers (although superior to you) and still more by men of your rank, even if he appears to have been impious towards divine things or found guilty of some other transgression. For this is to confuse distinctions and ranks, to overstep the most sacred commands and rights established by God. It is utterly unreasonable through a supposed zeal for God to overturn a divinely constituted order, for the word of God is not divided against itself, otherwise how should His Kingdom stand?[44] Although judgement belongs to God, as the Holy Scriptures testify, yet the priests are the messengers of the divine judgements, and rulers subordinate only to the bishop. As through them you have the privilege of divine worship, so through them and the ministers who aid them you learn, in due order, time and place, the revelation of God. Do not the sacred emblems themselves proclaim this truth ? For the sanctuary is not equally inaccessible to all, but the sacred dignity of the bishops has the closest approach, after them the order of priests, followed in turn by the ranks of the ministers.'

Philo, who is even said to have been of the household of St. Peter in Rome, in a book which he wrote concerning the life of contemplation and supplication, speaking of the Christians who dwelt around Alexandria, mentions holy ministers, priests and bishops, showing how the priests and ministers carried out their duties and how the episcopal chair was sovereign over all.[45]

St. Clement, finally, gives to James, Bishop of Jerusalem, a résumé of some points in St. Peter's daily teaching.[46] Amongst other things, he recalls how the apostle taught the duty of bishops, viz. that they should love their priests, the other ministers of the Church, and the people committed to their care, and should instruct them in God's words and commandments. All these in turn should love their bishops with all their heart as the very pupils of their eyes, as indeed they are. In all things they are to obey their commands, even though the bishops themselves (which God forbid) act otherwise, mindful of the command of our Lord: " Whatsoever they say unto you, observe and do, but according to their deeds do ye not." '[47]

From the unanimity of so many of the Fathers we may conclude with the fullest certainty that the priesthood was instituted, not in recent times, but in the very cradle of the Church. Wherefore, since Luther can adduce no orthodox writer who in any book that has ever appeared gives contrary witness, nor can quote a single syllable of Holy Scripture in opposition to the assertions of the Fathers, we lay down with the utmost justice against Luther as a matter of prescriptive right the truth of the priesthood.

The only point that Luther has for his heresy is that the New Testament never uses this term, i.e. it never gives the name ' priests ' to those to whom to-day we give it. But this will have little or no force for one who carefully weighs the reason why the apostles avoided the term, viz., because the ancient priesthood was still in existence and daily sacrifice was offered in the Temple. Therefore, so that there might be no confusion between the two priesthoods, they thought it wise for the time being to use other terms for the new priests. Therefore, as is clear from Scripture, they called them at one time presbyters, at another ministers, sometimes bishops and pastors, until that time when, together with the Temple, the ancient priesthood was utterly destroyed. After that occurred it became usual for all men to call our presbyters priests.

I would have you, dear reader, hold this as a most certain truth, that from the Scriptures Luther has not one jot or tittle which contradicts a visible priesthood, nor a single one of the orthodox prelates of the Church who even once gives any support to his teaching, but on the contrary that they all unanimously and emphatically testify the exact opposite.

Here, then, is our first rejoinder to Luther. Whereas the truth of the priesthood is abundantly and unanimously witnessed to by all the Fathers through the whole history of the Church, and whereas there is no orthodox writer who is not in agreement, and no word of Scripture that can be quoted against it, therefore all must clearly see how justly, against Luther, we claim the truth of the priesthood as the prescriptive right of the Church.

It would indeed be incredible that when Christ had redeemed His Church at so great a price, the price of His Precious Blood, He should care for it so little as to leave it enveloped in so black an error.

Nor is it any more credible that the Holy Ghost, who was sent for the special purpose of leading the Church into all truth, should allow it for so long to be led astray.

Nor is it credible that the prelates of the Church, who were so numerous even in the earliest period of her history and who were appointed by the Holy Ghost to rule her, as we shall afterwards prove, should have been enveloped in such darkness through so many centuries as to teach publicly so foul a lie.

Finally it is beyond all belief that so many churches throughout the various parts of Christendom, hitherto governed with such careful solicitude by Christ and His Spirit and by the prelates appointed for the purpose, should now unanimously fall into an error so foul and a lie so ruinous, according to Luther, that it does an injustice to the very testament of our Lord.

But consider diligently Christ's care for us: consider the certain truths of the presence and the activity of the Holy Spirit in the Church: consider the numberless clear testimonies of the prelates of olden times, illustrious not only by their holiness, but also by their learning and miracles: consider the unanimous agreement of all the churches, with no single exception through so many centuries. How now can it be imagined that at length for the first time has shone upon Luther the light of a truth that no one of the early Fathers could so much as have suspected, the contrary, indeed, of which they have unitedly asserted from the very beginning?

For if for so long the truth had remained imprisoned in darkness, waiting during so many centuries for Luther, and him only, to set it free, then Christ's solicitude for our Fathers in the faith was in vain; in vain, too, the coming of the Holy Ghost to teach them all truth; in vain their prayers and devout search for the truth, if all along they were unanimously teaching to the churches so dangerous a lie.

And if there was an error in a matter so vital to the faith, then in vain, if I may use the language of Tertullian,[48] were so many millions of men baptized, in vain were wrought so many works of faith and miracles, in vain so many graces given, so many functions of the priesthood performed, in vain did so many martrys suffer, if indeed they all died in a false faith. For without the true faith, no one of them could please God.[49]

Now that you see, dear reader, the source whence that doctrine has come unchanged down to us, i.e. from men of the greatest sanctity and learning, some of whom were of the apostolic age and undoubtedly received it from the apostles themselves, whereas Luther can quote nothing of the kind for his opinion, as we shall soon clearly show, who will be so reckless of his salvation as to leave these safe guides and endanger his soul with Luther? Who does not know that we must zealously follow the safer path, especially as it is written: 'He that loveth danger shall perish in it.'[50] And how shall not that path be safer which one follows in the company of the Fathers, so eminent in learning and holiness, than in opposition to all these in the company of Luther alone? He who follows the unanimous teaching of the Fathers, clearly follows the Church. But he who follows the Church, in any matter appertaining to the faith, cannot be deceived, for the Church is the pillar and the ground of the truth.[51] Therefore, the obviously safer way is to follow these Fathers; nor can anyone, without manifest peril to his soul, desert them and follow Luther.

Now when we follow the early Fathers, unanimous in their witness to the priesthood, we are following the Church, for what else was the Church, but a congregation composed entirely of prelates and subjects? And clearly, all these prelates from the beginning taught this doctrine, and all the subjects accepted it. Therefore there cannot be the slightest doubt that he who has believed this teaching has followed the Church. Undoubtedly, then, it must be considered the more secure way to follow the teaching of the Fathers against which no orthodox Catholic throughout the ages has protested, than to follow so notorious a heresiarch as Luther. For who can doubt that the early Fathers who received the command to teach, and who were appointed to that office by the Holy Ghost, were in fact taught the truth infallibly by that same Spirit? This we may conclude especially in regard to those doctrines about which there was never any controversy among them. Wherefore, he who shall take his stand with Luther against the Fathers, especially when Luther can quote for his side neither any clear text of Scripture, as we shall soon prove, nor the witness of any orthodox writer, he is clearly casting himself into a peril not doubtful but most evident.

So much for our first rejoinder.

Section 3

SECOND REJOINDER

Introduction

TO prove now the doctrine more adequately from Scripture, we shall try to establish certain axioms from which it will be most clearly seen that the office which we call the priesthood was not a human invention, as Luther would have it, but a divine institution.

To begin with, however, I will not quarrel about words, that is, about the name that should be given to those whom to-day we call priests. For it makes no difference for our present argument whether they be called priests or presbyters or pastors or anything else.

I undertake now to show how necessary it is that some men should stand between God and the people, to discharge in regard to the people the same duties which to-day we see the priests perform. And this I will show to be not invented by men but instituted by God. Now if this shall once appear evident from the Scriptures themselves, who shall be able to have any further doubt on the subject? For where the thing itself is certain, any dispute about names is idle.

§ 3] SECOND REJOINDER

But before we enunciate our axioms, let us hear what Luther has to say. Soon after the beginning of his book, he writes as follows: 'If you wish to be truly a Christian, be sure and allow no argument to persuade you otherwise, that there is no visible and external priesthood in the New Testament except what has been set up by Satan and lying men. Our one and only priesthood is the priesthood of Christ, by which He offered Himself for us, and all of us with Himself, as St. Peter says: " Christ died once for our sins, the just for the unjust, that He might offer us to God, being put to death indeed in the flesh, but brought to life by the Spirit."[1] And again the Epistle to the Hebrews: " For by one oblation He hath perfected for ever them that are sanctified."[2] This priesthood is spiritual and common to all Christians. For all we who are Christians, that is, sons of Christ, the great High Priest, are priests by the same priesthood as He. Nor have we need of any other priest or mediator but Christ.'

Here, dear reader, you hear Luther utterly condemning every priesthood which is visible and external, as being set up by Satan and lying men, and teaching that Christ alone is a priest in whom all Christians are also priests, and that they need absolutely no other priest nor mediator save Christ. The magnitude of his errors, as here expressed, will be clear from the axioms which follow.

Section 4

FIRST AXIOM

It is reasonable, in matters concerning the salvation of souls, that some men be set apart to act in the name of, and bear responsibility for, the whole multitude.

HOW needful this is may be seen in many ways, but now in particular on account of six special dangers to which the vast majority of Christians is certainly liable.

The first is the grave danger of falling away from the faith, of which St. Paul speaks in the first Epistle to Timothy: 'Some have made shipwreck concerning the faith,'[1] and again in the same place, 'Some have gone astray from a good conscience and an unfeigned faith.'[2] Often, too, St. Paul exhorts those to whom he writes to remain constant in faith, and sometimes blames them for falling away, for example, the Galatians. If, then, faith once received may be lost, clearly there is need of a guide, a pastor, who will 'preach the word, be instant in season, out of season, reprove, entreat, rebuke,' as St. Paul teaches Timothy.[3]

A second danger is the dullness of men's minds. Thus St. Paul had to rebuke the Corinthians as carnal, and little children in Christ, who had need of milk as they were not yet old enough to eat solid food.⁴ He addressed a similar rebuke to the Hebrews: 'You are become such as have need of milk, and not of solid food.'⁵ In no other way can this be understood than as referring to the dullness of their intellect, for immediately before he reproaches them with being weak to hear, and whereas for the time they ought to have been masters, they had need to be taught again what are the first rudiments of the word of God. Then again he calls the Galatians senseless.⁶ For they were of the race of the Gauls and, according to St. Jerome, gave evidence of their origin by the slowness of their intellects. Who, then, can deny that men of this kind needed a teacher?

A third danger is the facility with which men fall into every kind of sin. Again and again, St. Paul bears witness to this in regard to the Corinthians. For example, 'For I fear lest, when I come, I shall not find you such as I would, and that I shall be found by you such as you would not: lest perhaps contentions, envyings, animosities, dissensions, detractions, whisperings, swellings, seditions, be among you . . . and I bewail many of them that sinned before, and have not done penance for the uncleanness and fornication and lasciviousness that they have committed.'⁷

In the first Epistle he warns us all by the punishment of the Jews. 'Let us not covet evil things as they also coveted. Neither become ye idolaters, as some of them. . . . Neither let us commit fornication as some of them committed fornication, and there fell in one day three and twenty thousand. Neither let us tempt Christ, as some of them tempted, and perished by serpents. Neither do you murmur, as some of them murmured and were destroyed by the destroyer. Now all these things happened to them in figure, and they are written for our correction upon whom the ends of the world are come. Wherefore, let him that thinketh himself to stand take heed lest he fall.'[8] See, dear reader, how easily one may fall back into earlier sins. How necessary, then, it is to the people to have a monitor to strengthen them by his diligent exhortations, that they may not rush headlong into every kind of vice.

The fourth danger is man's sluggishness to good. A large proportion of Christians are commonly slothful to do good, and show much greater diligence in caring for their bodies than for the salvation of their souls. Not only now, but even in the very beginning of the Church, there were many such. Otherwise St. Paul would not have said to the Hebrews: 'Lift up the hands which hang down, and the feeble knees,'[9] nor blamed the Thessalonians for sloth,[10] nor accused the younger widows of idleness, as he does in writing to Timothy.[11] Nor would St. John in the Apocalypse have rebuked one for leaving his first charity,[12] nor have threatened another who was neither hot nor cold that God would begin to vomit him out of His mouth.[13] How many, alas, are lukewarm in these days of which our Lord foretold that as iniquity would abound so would the charity of many grow cold![14] How blind, then, is he who would deny that, to stir up the people from their lethargy, pastors and teachers are necessary!

The fifth danger is diabolic temptation. Of this

St. Paul often speaks, for instance to the Ephesians : ' Put ye on the whole armour of God, that ye may be able to stand against the snares of the devil. For our wrestling is not against flesh and blood, but against principalities and powers, against the rulers of the world of this darkness, against the spirits of wickedness in the high places.'[15] St. Peter, too, writes : ' Your adversary the devil, as a roaring lion, goeth about seeking whom he may devour.'[16] In the Apocalypse we are told that he seduces the whole world.[17] Our Saviour Himself, in St. Mark's Gospel, bears witness that Satan hinders the seed of the word of God from taking root in the hearts of many.[18] In St. Luke's Gospel, moreover, He says to Simon Peter : ' Behold, Satan hath desired to have you, that he may sift you as wheat.'[19] If then, the common adversary of mankind attacks even the holy apostles, how can the rank and file of Christians hope for immunity ? How necessary then, is the vigilant care of pastors that the people may be stirred up to defend themselves from his attacks.

The sixth is the poisonous errors of false teachers. Our Lord Himself bade us beware of such. ' Beware of false prophets,' He says, ' who come to you in the clothing of sheep, but inwardly they are ravenous wolves.'[20] And in another passage He foretells that they shall seduce many.[21] Thus, too, the Romans had been led astray, but St. Paul brought them back to the right rule of faith. The Corinthians, too, were warned by him against false teachers. The Galatians, also, who had been bewitched by them.[22] With many words, too, does he beseech the Philippians and Colossians to avoid them. Again, writing to Timothy, he says that Hymeneus and Alexander have erred in the faith and have led others astray.[23] So, too, does he urge the bishops of the Ephesians to vigilance against them. 'Take heed to yourselves, and to all the flock, over which the Holy Ghost hath placed you bishops, to rule the Church of God, which He hath purchased with His own blood. I know that after my departure ravenous wolves will enter in among you, not sparing the flock, and of your own selves will rise up men speaking perverse things, to draw away disciples after them.'[24]

Evidently, then, on account of the six dangers of which we have spoken, pastors and teachers are most necessary to the Christian flock, as long as we are in this world exiled from Christ.

Section 5

SECOND AXIOM

Christ Himself, whilst He was on earth, put certain pastors in charge of His flock, to watch over, rule, and teach it.

ST. LUKE relates how Christ, after He had spent the whole night in prayer to His Father, when it was day called His disciples and chose from them twelve whom He named apostles.[1] Note diligently, dear reader, with what careful preparation Christ selected them, spending the entire night in unbroken prayer before He appointed them to the office.

St. Mark relates the matter thus: ' Jesus, going up into a mountain, called unto Him whom He would Himself, and they came to Him. And He made that twelve should be with Him, and that He might send them to preach.'[2]

From these texts it may be seen that the apostles were chosen and appointed with great care and that to them were committed an office more exalted and an authority more extensive than to the rest of the disciples, as we shall show more fully in our fourth axiom.

Moreover, St. Matthew, after enumerating the

twelve apostles, adds: 'These twelve Jesus sent, and commanded them saying: Go not into the way of the Gentiles, and into the cities of the Samaritans enter not, but go rather to the lost sheep of the house of Israel. And going preach, saying: The kingdom of heaven is at hand.'[3] See how He committed to their care the sheep of the house of Israel and wished them to teach them.

St. John, too, may be quoted. He records how Christ said to them: 'Have I not chosen you twelve?'[4]; and again: 'You have not chosen Me, but I have chosen you, and have appointed you that you should go, and should bring forth fruit, and your fruit should remain.'[5] By 'fruit' He obviously means especially the salvation of souls, for it was to guide, to govern and to teach these that He appointed the apostles. Not only were the Jews committed to their care, but not long after the Gentiles also. For when He was about to ascend into heaven, He commanded them to go into the whole world and teach all nations, as both St. Matthew and St. Mark testify.

But in an especial way He appointed St. Peter, after He had thrice asked him whether he loved Him, the chief pastor of His flock. This is related by St. John in the last chapter of his Gospel. 'When therefore they had dined, Jesus saith to Simon Peter: Simon, son of John, lovest thou Me more than these? He saith to Him: Yea, Lord, Thou knowest that I love Thee. He saith to him: Feed My lambs. He saith to him again: Simon, son of John, lovest thou Me? He saith to Him: Yea, Lord, Thou knowest that I love Thee. He saith to him: Feed My lambs. He said to him the third time : Simon, son of John, lovest thou Me? Peter was grieved because He said to him the third time, Lovest thou Me? And he said to Him: Lord, Thou knowest all things, Thou knowest that I love Thee. He said to him: Feed My sheep.'[6] It is, then, as clear as day that Christ appointed these twelve pastors to watch over His flock, and that they were not only to teach, but to rule and, if necessary, to correct it. Otherwise St. Paul would not from time to time have used the rod of correction, nor would he have said to Titus, whom he placed in authority over the Cretans: 'For this cause I left thee in Crete, that thou shouldest set in order the things that are wanting.'[7]

In addition, too, to the apostles there were appointed by our Lord seventy-two disciples, as St. Luke writes. These were chosen out from the rest of the disciples and given special authority. For to them it was commanded to heal the sick and to work in the vineyard of the Lord, going out two by two into every city and place where our Lord was about to come. If any city would not receive them, Christ threatened that it would be more tolerable for Sodom in the day of judgement than for that city. If any one should despise them, it would be the same as if he despised Christ, and if any one should hear them, as if he heard Christ. To them also, he gave power over the devils, over serpents and scorpions, and over all the power of the enemy.[8] From these words it clearly appears that to them was given authority to teach, together with some responsibility for the flock, although not equal with the twelve apostles.

Thus it is evident that the twelve apostles stand

far apart from the seventy-two disciples, as do these in turn from the general body of the disciples. Now we cannot think that Christ wished this variety of orders to be a purely temporary measure, but rather that He wished it to last so long as the Church Militant should endure upon earth, as we shall show more clearly later on. Meanwhile, it is obvious that it was not without cause that our fathers in the faith perpetuated this distinction, so that there should be some to take the place of the apostles, some that of the disciples. We cannot but think that this was done by the guidance of the Holy Ghost, especially as the example had first been given to them by Christ. Surely not even the most outrageous heretic would deny that distinction of ranks to have been ordained by Christ. That being so, he must admit also that these ranks cannot belong to every individual member of the Church, but that certain ones must be appointed to them by those to whom our Lord committed such authority. But of this, more hereafter. Clearly, then, what has been handed down to us by tradition is quite reasonable, viz. that those who have succeeded the apostles and hold the higher rank should be called bishops or greater priests, whilst those who have succeeded the seventy-two disciples and hold the second rank should be called presbyters or lesser priests. We shall have more to say on this matter, but for the present we have said enough on our second axiom.

Section 6

THIRD AXIOM

It is fitting that those who are thus appointed pastors of the Christian flock should receive more abundant gifts of grace than others.

OF the truth of this axiom no one can doubt who will regard the order of created things in the universe. Here it can be seen that the superior bodies whom God uses as His instruments to rule the inferior bodies are gifted with greater powers than the latter. For since it was ordained by God that these lower things, prone as they were to corruption and death, should be maintained in being, therefore did He will that there should be higher things of greater stability which by their influence and virtue should ensure renewal and life to the others. For this purpose then, He gave resplendent powers to these superior bodies, so that they bestow light, heat, moisture, life, thunder and lightning.

Similar influences did God establish in His Church, which is a kind of spiritual universe with spiritual heavens and earth. Therefore, in the Psalm, David, seeing by the inspiration of the Spirit the future order and constitution of the Church, compares the apostles and other ministers of God in the Church to the heavens, the people to the earth. 'The heavens,' he says, 'tell forth the glory of God.'[1] For as the heavenly bodies in their orbits give light, heat, moisture, life, thunder and lightning, so do the apostles and other ministers carry out analogous offices. They give light by the example of their lives, heat by the fervour of their charity, moisture by their exhortations, life by the greatness of their promises, thunder by their warnings, lightning by their miracles, so that fittingly does David in the same Psalm say of them: 'Their sound hath gone forth into the whole earth.'[2] Since then the Church remains ever whole and entire, and needs now such ministries just as in the times of the apostles, so, too, is it still necessary that those who fill the places of the apostles, should be adorned with gifts proportionate to their ministry.

Another illustration can be drawn from the human body, which is a copy of the order of the universe. The senses, bestowed upon man for the utility of the whole body, have correspondingly greater delicacy. And even amongst the senses those that are nobler are also finer. The sense of touch, for example, which is more coarse and gross than the others, since it is like the earth, can distinguish only those things with which it is in immediate contact. The sense of taste, a little nobler and clearer, like the clearness of water, gives judgement of things that are slightly further away. The sense of smell, already higher and finer, like to the delicacy of a cloud, can exert its powers over a far wider space. Far nobler and purer is the sense of hearing, which represents the clarity and immateriality of the air and detects sounds from a still greater distance. Lastly the sight, as it has the highest position in the body, has also the most extensive range and represents the beauty of the skies. Brilliant itself, the eye can exert its power of sight over the vastest spaces.

As therefore in the body of man those senses which are nobler are endowed with superior powers, so, too, in the body of the Church, those members which rule the others receive more abundant gifts of grace from God. Of this we shall say more in the next axiom.

But let us support our contention from Holy Scripture. When Moses was overwhelmed with anxiety and nearly sank under his burden, unable to govern so numerous a multitude, God said to him: ' Gather unto me seventy men of the ancients of Israel, whom thou knowest to be ancients and masters of the people; and thou shalt bring them to the door of the tabernacle of the covenant, and thou shalt make them stand there with thee, that I may come down and speak with thee: and I will take of thy spirit, and will give to them, that they may bear with thee the burden of the people, and thou mayst not be burthened alone.'[3] And so it was done. If God showed such care for the old synagogue—now superseded—as to confer such a grace upon its rulers, how much more suitably does He do so for the Church, which is gathered together from the multitudes of the Gentiles, redeemed by the blood of Christ and made His spouse. It is now wandering in the desert of this world and for the government of its vast multitudes it needs many pastors. Surely, then, it is fitting that the burden of its rule should be distributed among many, and that they should be more abundantly endowed with the graces of the Holy Spirit, that they may the more fruitfully exercise their office.

Again when God willed the tabernacle of the covenant to be built in the desert and no skilled workmen could be found to erect it, He filled a certain Beseleel, the son of Hur, with the Spirit of God, and enriched him ' with wisdom, understanding and knowledge, to devise in each work what should be made of gold, silver, brass, marble, precious stones and variety of wood,' to whom He gave as his companion Ooliab, the son of Achisamech.[4] Can it be imagined that God would do so much for the tabernacle of the covenant which is now swept away, and yet not trouble to appoint overseers for the great work, still daily proceeding, of building up the tabernacle of the mystical body of Christ, nor adorn them with the necessary virtues? Such a supposition would be utterly at variance with all that we know of the goodness of God, who, when He proposes to carry out some work, never fails to provide the means necessary for attaining His end.

Section 7

FOURTH AXIOM

Not only was it fitting that Christ should do so, but in fact He did bestow upon such pastors of His Church grace and power suitably to discharge their duties.

CHRIST chose His twelve apostles from the common people, rude and unlettered men, to say no more; but when He placed them as rulers over His flock, He endowed them with the richest graces. Thus St. Matthew writes that 'He gave them power over unclean spirits, to cast them out, and to heal all manner of diseases and all manner of sicknesses.'[1] He relates, too, how they received such wisdom that they needed not to take thought beforehand what they should speak. 'It shall be given to you in that hour what to speak, for it is not you that speak, but the Spirit of your Father that speaketh in you.'[2] Though in addition this gift may afterwards have been enjoyed by many others, yet it is clear enough that it is in this passage specially promised to the apostles. So, too, St. Luke says: 'Jesus, having called together the twelve apostles, gave them power and authority over all devils and to cure diseases. And He sent them to preach the kingdom of God and to heal the sick.'³ St. Mark relates that 'going forth they preached penance, and they cast out many devils and anointed with oil many that were sick and healed them.'⁴ How could this be done, I ask, without extraordinary gifts of grace?

Moreover, we learn from St. Mark that the reason why Christ chose the Twelve was that they might always be with Him.⁵ What does this mean but that beyond all the rest they were brought into close intimacy with Him and enjoyed greater authority than the others. Moreover, these sat at table with Him at the Last Supper and received from Him the power of consecrating His body. According to St. Luke, 'When the hour was come, He sat down, and the twelve apostles with Him. And He said to them: With desire I have desired to eat this pasch with you before I suffer. . . . And taking bread, He gave thanks, and brake, and gave to them, saying: This is My body which is given for you; do this for a commemoration of Me.'⁶ Note how it was to the Twelve He gave the power of consecrating His body. For we can infer from the same Evangelist that no others were present but Christ and the Twelve, for clearly one cup would not have been sufficient for more. But Jesus, as St. Luke tells us, took the cup and said to those at table: 'Take and divide it among you.'

In addition, it was to these same apostles that long before He suffered He gave the power of binding and loosing, as St. Matthew narrates.⁷ Now Luther has never shown that this power was given to any but the apostles. St. John, too, testifies that after His Resurrection Christ breathed upon them, bestowed on them the Holy Spirit together with the power of forgiving sins. 'As the Father hath sent Me, I also send you. When He had said this He breathed upon them and He said to them: Receive ye the Holy Ghost: Whose sins ye shall forgive, they are forgiven them, and whose sins ye shall retain, they are retained.'[8] Luther cannot object here that these words were directed to all Christians, for it is clear that not all Christians were sent by Christ. But these words were uttered for those alone who were sent. 'As the Father hath sent Me,' He says, 'I also send you.'

St. Luke makes the matter clear in the opening words of the Acts of the Apostles. 'The former treatise I made, O Theophilus, of all things which Jesus began to do and to teach, until the day on which, bestowing the Holy Ghost for this very purpose and giving commands to the apostles whom He had chosen, He was taken up.'[9] These words show not only that Christ chose the apostles, but that He gave them special commands and this after He had bestowed upon them the Holy Ghost to help them to observe these commands. What these commands were St. Mark shows. 'He appeared to the Eleven as they were at table, and He upbraided them with their incredulity and hardness of heart, because they did not believe them who had seen Him after He was risen again. And He said to them: Go ye into the whole world, and preach the gospel to every creature.'[10] St. Matthew relates the same commission thus: 'Go ye therefore and teach all nations, baptizing them in the name of the Father, and of the Son, and of the Holy Ghost.'[11] The command therefore that He gave them was that they were to go through the world, teach and baptize in the name of the Father and of the Son and of the Holy Ghost.

Now Luther accepts nothing but what is in the Gospel. Let him show, then, from the Gospel that this commission was given to all and we will believe him. But if he cannot, but on the contrary, demands that we shall believe his words without warrant from the Gospel, all can see how utterly unfair that is.

So, dear reader, you see how Christ gave to His apostles special privileges and graces, together with authority over others, that they might fulfil more easily and more perfectly the task He had laid upon them. The seventy disciples, too, received gifts which though not so elevated as those granted to the apostles yet were far beyond what was given to the rank and file of the people. Enough, then, for this fourth axiom.

Section 8

FIFTH AXIOM

The institution of pastors not only was necessary in the early days of the Church's life but needs to last for ever, until the building-up of the Church is fully completed.

WE proved in our book against Velenus[1] that the succession of pastors which began in Christ is not to be ended until the fulfilment of all that Christ foretold. So did He testify in the Gospel: 'This age shall not pass away until all these things be fulfilled.'[2] But it will be clear to anyone who will read that discourse that some of Christ's prophecies have not yet been verified. Therefore the succession of this age is far yet from being finished, but is to be continued from the same source whence it began.

Again, Christ promised His apostles and disciples that as long as the world lasted He would not fail them. 'Behold I am with you all days, even to the consummation of the world.'[3] Clearly this assurance was given not only for those then present, but also for all their descendants; for those who were then living and those who have followed them up to this time form as it were one age and one lasting generation.

But St. Paul will make this lesson still clearer. He writes to the Ephesians: 'Christ gave some to be apostles, and some prophets, and others evangelists, and others pastors and teachers.' But to what purpose? 'For the perfection of the saints, for the work of the ministry, unto the edification of the body of Christ.' But how long will that last? 'Till we all meet in the unity of faith, and of the knowledge of the Son of God, unto a perfect man, unto the measure of the age of the fulness of Christ.' And when shall that be? 'When we cease to be children, tossed to and fro, and carried about with every wind of doctrine, in the wickedness of men, in craftiness by which they lie in wait to deceive.'[4] Thus, dear reader, so long as you see Christians tossed and carried about with every wind of doctrine by the wickedness of men, by the craftiness by which they lie in wait to deceive us, so long you may be sure that we have not all arrived at the unity of faith and knowledge of the Son of God, that we have not grown unto the perfect man nor unto the measure of the age of the fulness of Christ. Wherefore the building-up of the Body of Christ, that is the Church, is not yet completed. Clearly, then, there is need for the continuance of the Church's pastors.

St. Paul's words make it quite evident that certain men must be appointed in the Church to take the place of the apostles, others of the prophets, the evangelists, the pastors and the doctors, and that upon them is bestowed grace more abundant than upon the rest, according to the measure of the gift of Christ. This, too, is to continue unbrokenly until the Church is fully edified and consummated.

For St. Paul teaches that the Church will ever be adorned by a variety of gifts. 'For as in one body we have many members, but all the members have not the same office, so we, being many, are one body in Christ and each one members one of another. Having gifts different, according to the grace that is given us, whether prophecy, according to the proportion of faith; or ministry in ministering; or he that teacheth in teaching; he that exhorteth in exhorting; he that giveth with simplicity; he that ruleth with solicitude; he that showeth mercy with cheerfulness.'[5] With gifts of such variety will the body of the Church ever be adorned. Therefore he teaches the Corinthians that not all are apostles, nor prophets, nor teachers, nor workers of miracles, that not all have the grace of healing, nor speak with tongues, nor interpret; but that amongst the members of the Church there are many divisions, not of gifts alone, but also of ministries and operations.[6]

For God in His goodness and wisdom will never fail to provide the means which are necessary for the end He desires, as can be clearly seen in the examples we quoted in support of our third axiom. For when God willed the succession of inferior bodies in this universe to be perpetuated He endowed the superior or heavenly bodies with such powers as would ensure that succession. So, too, in the human body He provided certain members with more excellent endowments for the health and comfort of the whole. A similar method did He adopt in the body of His Church which He willed to be built up gradually by men's toils and devotion. For this reason did He wish various ranks of men to be established in His Church and to each assign appropriate gifts. For it would be idle for any man to attempt to contribute anything towards the building-up of this body unless God had endowed him with special powers for the purpose. And even if he had received such powers he would not bring forth abundant fruit unless also he had been legitimately sent. 'For how,' says St. Paul, 'shall they preach unless they be sent?'[7] He who wishes to be of use must be sent and duly appointed to his office. It often happens that a preacher who is less learned does more good to his hearers than one who is far more learned. This can only be because the one is assisted by a special gift of grace. For one who is duly sent receives the grace of the Holy Ghost, and indeed in a much more intimate manner than he received it once in Baptism.

Section 9

SIXTH AXIOM

No one rightly exercises the pastoral office unless he be called, and duly receive from the prelates of the Church both ordination and mission.

AS to vocation, St. Paul speaks of its necessity in the Epistle to the Hebrews: 'No man taketh the honour to himself but he that is called by God, as Aaron was. So also Christ did not glorify Himself to be made a high priest, but He that said to Him: Thou art My Son, this day have I begotten Thee. As He saith also in another place: Thou art a priest for ever according to the order of Melchisedech.'[1] So that if Christ, the first pastor, did not arrogate the honour, nor glorify Himself that He might become a priest, much less is it lawful to others. No one, then, may claim the honour of pastor unless he be duly called by God. We have the example of the first pastors who were called, one by one, by Christ, whereas the Scribe who offered himself uncalled was repulsed by Him.[2] God, as we see from St. Luke's Gospel, does not bestow His gifts except upon those whom He calls. 'Calling,' He says, 'his ten servants, he delivered to them ten pounds.'[3]

Note how the pounds were given to those who were called. St. Paul, too, claimed to be an apostle because of the call of Christ.⁴ St. Matthias, again, did not put himself forward, but was chosen after the apostles had prayed and cast lots, and thus he was made of their number.⁵ The apostles had not yet received the Holy Ghost nor had been instructed by Him what rite they should adopt for ordinations.

But St. Paul, though he had been personally called by Christ, yet at the bidding of the Holy Spirit was afterwards ordained, together with Barnabas. For, as we read in the Acts of the Apostles, there were prophets and doctors at Antioch, offering sacrifice to God and fasting, when they were commanded by the Spirit to separate Barnabas and Saul, then present amongst them. 'Separate Me Barnabas and Saul for the work to which I have taken them.' The prophets and doctors, then, who had received this command 'fasting and praying, and imposing their hands upon Barnabas and Saul, sent them away.' And note how these two, thus sent away by them, were said to have been sent by the Holy Ghost. 'So they, being sent by the Holy Ghost, went away.'⁶ Now the work to which they were summoned was not only the conversion of the people to Christ, but also the appointment and ordination of priests for the churches. Thus in the fourteenth chapter of the Acts we find the word χειροτονήσαντες, which means 'when *by the imposition of hands they had ordained* for the people priests in every church, and had prayed with fasting, they commended them to the Lord.'⁷ And then we read that they returned to Antioch 'from whence they had been delivered to the grace of God unto the work which they accomplished.'

Weigh all this, dear reader, carefully and if I am not mistaken you will see how far Luther has departed from the truth. I will not speak now of the liturgy or what the Fathers call sacrificing.[8] Note, however, that these two saintly men, Barnabas and Saul, though they were chosen by the Holy Ghost, were yet made priests, by the prophets and doctors, by fasting, prayer and the imposition of hands. Note secondly that the work to which they were ordained was not simply the ministry of the word but the ordaining of other priests in turn for every church. Note thirdly that the ceremonies they used for ordaining priests were the same, viz. the laying-on of hands, prayer and fasting. Note lastly that until they had done this the ministry entrusted to them was not completed. For it was only when they had performed all these things fully that St. Luke relates their return to Antioch ' from whence they had been delivered to the grace of God unto the work ' (he says) ' which they accomplished.'[9]

It is clear then that as Barnabas and Saul were themselves called, ordained and sent, so in turn they called, ordained and sent many others. But why need I labour the point? Christ Himself called, appointed and sent the first apostles. St. Mark relates it briefly: ' Jesus going up into a mountain, called unto Him whom He would Himself.' Here is the call. ' And He made that twelve should be with Him.' Here is the appointment: ' And that He might send them to preach.'[10] Here is the sending: If anyone is not thus called, ordained and sent, he 'entereth not by the door into the sheepfold,' nor does the 'porter open to him,' but he is 'a thief and a robber.'[11] For he comes not with Christ's but with his own authority, and all such are undoubtedly thieves and robbers. 'All,' He says, 'who have come before Me,' i.e. on their own authority and before the call of Christ 'have broken into the fold and are thieves and robbers.'[12]

It is, then, the clear teaching of the Bible that no one can lawfully exercise the pastoral office unless he be duly called, ordained and sent by the prelates of the Church. Neither can Luther in honour disagree, for he has himself subscribed to it. Thus in his commentary on the Epistle to the Galatians he writes: 'All this is said that you may appreciate the care Christ showed in establishing and protecting His Church, that no one should rashly presume to teach unless he be sent by Christ Himself or by those sent by Christ.' Luther, then, fully subscribes to our axiom and we need reason no further about it.

Section 10

Seventh Axiom

Those who are lawfully appointed by the pastors of the Church to the pastoral office are undoubtedly called also by the Holy Ghost.

WE have already shown that the rite or method by which new priests were to be ordained was chosen by the Holy Ghost Himself. For as there were at Antioch prophets and doctors, fasting and offering sacrifice, and amongst them Barnabas and Saul, the Holy Ghost commanded them to separate these two for the ministry to which He called them. Note that though they were called to the apostolic ministry by the Holy Ghost, yet He commanded that they should be separated by the prophets and doctors who were there present. Now if this word 'separate' means no more than 'send,' why did these prophets and doctors use so many idle ceremonies? For they fasted, prayed and laid hands upon them before they sent them away. Obviously then it was by this rite that they were made apostles.

Nor let anyone bring it forward as an objection that St. Paul had already been called by Christ. For there are the clearest proofs, both in this very passage and elsewhere, that it was only at this time that he was made an apostle. One proof is that St. Luke, though so devoted a friend of St. Paul, in writing his history never before this time calls him Paul, but Saul always. But now, as soon as Saul is separated for the apostolate, St. Luke always calls him Paul.¹

Another proof, and a strong one, is that St. Luke puts Saul after all the others, in the very last place. 'There were in the church which was at Antioch prophets and teachers, among whom was Barnabas, and Simon who was called Niger, and Lucius of Cyrene, and Manahen who was the foster-brother of Herod the tetrarch, and Saul.'² St. Luke would certainly not have put Saul thus in the last place if he had already been regarded as an apostle. For apostles are not to be placed after prophets and teachers, as St. Paul himself testifies, saying: 'First apostles, secondly prophets.'³

A third proof is that nowhere else do we read that St. Barnabas was made an apostle, and yet we know that he was an apostle and considered as such by all. Wherefore if at this time St. Barnabas was created an apostle why should we not say the same of St. Paul, since it is obvious that they are here both called to the same kind of ministry.

A fourth proof. What need was there otherwise that in sending out these two the others should fast, pray and impose hands? For by the imposition of hands grace is conferred, as we read in many places, even in the Acts themselves.

The last proof is that they received then the power of appointing and ordaining priests by the imposition of their hands, 'χειροτονήσαντες δὲ αὐτοῖς πρεσβυτέρους κατ' ἐκκλησίαν,'⁴ i.e. by the imposition of hands they ordained them priests in every church. Nor did they alone lay on hands, but they fasted and prayed, as is stated in the same passage. By fasting, prayer and the laying-on of hands, therefore, they consecrated priests and placed them in authority over the people. And that we may understand that this was a substantial part of the task enjoined on them it is added that they returned to Antioch 'whence they had been delivered to the grace of God unto the work which they accomplished.'⁵ The making of priests was therefore a part of the task and ministry entrusted to them at Antioch, for not until they had in this manner ordained priests was their ministry finished. Note, too, the expression of St. Luke, that they were 'delivered to the grace of God.' For who can doubt that when, at the command of the Holy Ghost, they were ordained so carefully, i.e. by prayer, fasting and the laying-on of hands, by the prophets and teachers, they received the richest graces of that same Spirit?

But further, St. Paul, writing to the Romans, glories in being thus set apart, 'Separated,' he says, 'unto the gospel of God.'⁶ Yet though they were sent in this manner, the sacred text makes it quite clear that they were sent out by the Holy Ghost Himself.

Perhaps you will ask why St. Matthias was not ordained in this manner. Clearly because the Holy Ghost had not yet come. He afterwards taught this rite which later on was observed commonly in all cases. For, as we have seen, Paul and Barnabas ordained priests in every church by fasting, prayer and the laying-on of hands. Need I say more? Of all the priests who were in this manner ordained, either by Barnabas and Paul, or by others possessed of similar authority, St. Paul did not hesitate to affirm that they were appointed by the Holy Ghost, and for the special purpose of ruling the Church of God. Thus many of the priests of Ephesus came to him and he addressed them in these words: 'Take heed to yourselves, and to all the flock, over which the Holy Ghost hath placed you bishops to rule the Church of God.'[7] Although they were appointed to this office by the hands of men yet St. Paul does not hesitate to attribute it to the Holy Ghost and to call it the work of God. Therefore as many as were ordained pastors in the lawful manner either by the apostles or by their successors were appointed by the Holy Ghost. But as this age or succession lasts, as we have said, not only to our own day but is to last to the end of the world, it follows that all who are or shall be duly called and ordained by the prelates of the Church to this office are to be regarded as appointed by the Holy Ghost Himself who abides for ever in the Church. So much for the seventh axiom.

Section 11

EIGHTH AXIOM

All those lawfully ordained receive from the Holy Ghost gifts of grace by which they are made more fit worthily to carry out the duties of their ministry.

NO one denies that St. Timothy was appointed bishop by St. Paul, and therefore we will draw our first argument from the Epistle the latter wrote to the former. 'Neglect not,' he writes, ' the grace which is in thee, which was given thee by prophecy with the imposition of the hands of the priesthood.'[1] Timothy, then, by the authority of that priesthood which belonged to the one who ordained him, received the gift of grace. That St. Paul himself was the one who ordained him appears in the Second Epistle to Timothy: ' I admonish thee that thou stir up the grace of God, which is in thee by the imposition of my hands.'[2] Here, then, St. Paul reveals himself as the one who ordained Timothy, and a second time asserts that at his ordination Timothy received the gift of grace. Ordination was always conferred by the laying-on of hands, as we shall afterwards show. Nor can we doubt that as St. Paul asserts that Timothy received grace, so he would say too of all others who should receive ordination from others enjoying equal authority with himself. We shall show, moreover, in the following axiom that this grace was given at the moment of Timothy's ordination and not, as Luther tries to argue, when he was baptized by St. Paul.

Nor was such grace given to Timothy alone, but also to Titus, and to all others who in turn were ordained by them. In general to all who were ordained by the apostles, or by those who had themselves been ordained by the apostles, grace was given, provided that those so ordained put no hindrance in the way. For what else could be an obstacle to the abundant grace of the Spirit? Is not the Holy Ghost the ever-flowing fount of the very richest graces? Is it not the very purpose of His abiding presence in the Church that He should bestow grace for the building-up of the spiritual edifice of the Church? Thus St. Paul teaches that to each one of us is given grace, but in one measure to the apostles, another to the prophets, another to the evangelists, another to the pastors and teachers. The purpose, however, of the grace which is thus given to all is ' for the perfection of the saints, for the work of the ministry, unto the edification of the body of Christ,'[3] which is the Church. St. Paul calls himself an architect,[4] for he received grace for the purpose of building-up the Church. But as that building is still far from complete other architects are needed, and they, too, like St. Paul, must receive graces for its edification. When the tabernacle of the covenant was being built, as we have before said, the Holy Ghost filled certain men ' with wisdom, understanding and knowledge to devise in each work what should best be made.'⁵ Such generosity characterized the Holy Ghost even before the time had come for pouring out the plenitude of His grace. But now that the Holy Ghost has been given, and given indeed for the very purpose of building-up the Church, surely He will not so much despise those whom He Himself has appointed to work at the erection of the edifice as to give them no grace. No one but Luther would ever believe such a thing.

Not, of course, that I deny that the people also have received grace, but, as is fitting, they receive it in a different measure to their pastors and rulers. Rulers and people differ, in the mind of St. Paul, as the architect differs from his house and the husbandman from his field. For he says: ' We are God's coadjutors.'⁶ If, then, he calls himself and the other rulers of the Church God's fellow-workers, what does he call the people? Not fellow-workers, but rather the material on which the work is done. For to the people he says: ' You are God's husbandry; you are God's building,' i.e. the husbandry and building of God whose fellow-workers he calls himself and the other rulers of the Church. For although God is the chief husbandman, yet the rulers of the Church are also called husbandmen in Holy Scripture. Thus in St. Matthew's Gospel we read: ' He will bring these evil men to an evil end, and will let out his vineyard to other husbandmen that shall render him the fruit in due season.'⁷ That is to say, under the Old Law the husbandmen were the ministers of that Law, whom, as they were evil, the lord of the vineyard brought to an evil end. But now under the Gospel God lets out His vineyard to other husbandmen to cultivate, who will bring Him, as He says, the fruit in due season. But the husbandmen to whom God's vineyard is let out are obviously the rulers of the Church. Now so long as the earlier husbandmen proved themselves worthy of the grace of the Holy Ghost, they received it. For, as we have said above, when Moses alone was not able to govern so vast a multitude he chose seventy elders whom God made to partake of the same Spirit as Moses, that they might be more fit to rule the people. Can we think that God did so much for the husbandmen of that people which He foresaw He would have to cast off, and yet gave nothing of the Spirit of Christ to the husbandmen whom He appointed to rule the people which He redeemed by the blood of His Son?

Again, under the Old Law not merely the High Priest but also the minor priests who held authority in the Temple were anointed in their ordination. Wherefore if the reality is to correspond with the shadow, as of course it should, then all who are ordained pastors of the Church at the hands of prelates must receive interiorly the spiritual unction of grace. For the grace of the Holy Ghost is a kind of spiritual anointing.

Here Luther breaks in and claims that that anointing is common to all Christians, and therefore that every Christian is a priest. Christ, he says, is the High Priest, but all other Christians are lesser priests.

But here Luther deceives both himself and others. For if Christ is our High Priest, and all other Christians are lesser priests, what are we to say of the people? If the reality is to correspond to its shadow, besides the High Priest and the people, there must be lesser priests to act as mediators between the High Priest and the people. Now if every Christian were a priest he would not be in authority over the Church, nor be a priest for the people, but for himself alone. But we now are speaking of priests who are priests for the people and are duly placed in authority over churches, such as those who, as we have above shown, must be called, ordained, and sent out to their ministry. But not all Christians are thus individually called, ordained and sent, and therefore they are not priests of this kind.

But we do not wish to deny that all Christians are anointed; anointed, however, to fight, not to preach the Gospel. Christ showed that He was anointed to preach the Gospel when he applied to Himself the prophecy of Isaias. 'The Spirit of the Lord is upon Me: wherefore He hath appointed Me to preach the Gospel to the poor.'[8] Christ, then, was spiritually anointed by grace that He might preach to the poor. But such an anointing priests alone share with Christ, for that they may more successfully fulfil their office of preaching, they receive the internal unction of the Holy Ghost. Such priests are priests not for themselves alone but for the people: they are lawfully placed over churches, being duly called, ordained and sent. Who now can doubt that they receive grace from the origin and giver of all graces, the Holy Spirit, by whom pastors, architects and husbandmen are provided for the people and for the Church of God?

Section 12

NINTH AXIOM

The Holy Spirit willed that grace should be attached to an outward sensible sign so that when the sign is duly performed we know by faith that grace is at the same moment bestowed.

THOUGH the Holy Scriptures do not teach this axiom in so many words, yet it is an obvious conclusion from what is therein contained. For the Scriptures do not always express truths which nevertheless we all believe undoubtedly to be such. For example, where is it written either that Christ taught his apostles or that the Holy Ghost commanded them to impose hands upon such as were baptized? And yet we read that they did it, and not fruitlessly. For when at the preaching of Philip the deacon the Samaritans believed and were baptized, they did not receive the Holy Ghost in a visible way before Peter and John had imposed hands upon them. Wherefore Simon, who by his magical art had beguiled the people, seeing that by the hands of the apostles the Holy Ghost was given, tried to buy this power for himself so that upon whomsoever he might impose hands that one might receive the Holy Ghost.[1] Now no one would believe that the apostles would thus have acted unless they had been before instructed by the Holy Ghost, and yet Scripture contains no word of their having thus been instructed.

There are certainly, then, many things which the apostles taught the Church but never committed to the Holy Scriptures. Eusebius of Cæsarea is a witness to this fact. He writes: ' When Ignatius, as a captive, was sailing along the coast of Asia and visiting the various cities, he preached the Gospel to the people of the Church and bade them remain firm in faith, guard themselves against the pestilential errors of the heretics, which then were beginning to be propagated, and hold carefully and steadily to the traditions of the apostles, which traditions, for the sake of safety and in order that there might be no uncertainty in future times, he says that he had left behind him in writing.'[2]

If only that book were still extant, in which Ignatius collected together the traditions of the apostles, it is certain that it would supply much that is now lacking. But to return to our point. As it was clearly by the instruction of the Holy Ghost that the apostles, by the laying-on of hands, bestowed the Holy Ghost upon those who were baptized, so it was by the command of the same Spirit that they laid hands upon those who were to be ordained, in order that they might receive a special grace for the due fulfilment of their office. Neither of these facts can be doubted by any Christian, for they are so plainly contained in Holy Scripture, although no record remains of an express command to the apostles.

That ordination was given by the imposition of

hands is clear from many passages of Scripture. We need not here repeat the two texts from St. Paul's Epistles to Timothy which we quoted at the opening of the proof of our eighth axiom.

There is no ground for Luther's objection that this imposition of hands was performed when Timothy was baptized by St. Paul. For hands were twice imposed upon him, as the Acts relate in regard to St. Paul himself. For when Paul was baptized by Ananias hands were imposed upon him[3] and a second time by the prophets and teachers when by command of the Spirit he was separated to the apostolate.[4] So also hands were twice imposed upon Timothy, once, as is the common use, after the reception of baptism, but of this the Scripture says nothing; a second time when he was ordained bishop, and of this St. Paul speaks. For from the context of the passage it is apparent that the gift of which St. Paul speaks was given to Timothy for the instruction of the people. 'Till I come, attend to reading, to exhortation and to doctrine.'[5] This is the introduction to the passage in question. Hence the imposition of hands to which St. Paul refers is obviously the ordination to the episcopate.

We may add that Luther has never shown from the Scriptures that Timothy was baptized by St. Paul. That he was circumcised by him we do not deny,[6] but that he was baptized by him is nowhere found in the Bible. If Luther wishes to adduce any testimony that is not in the Scriptures he is acting unfairly, for when it tells against him he will not admit any such evidence. In fact St. Paul baptized but rarely, for, as he says in the Epistle to the

Corinthians, ' Christ sent me not to baptize but to preach the Gospel.'[7] Moreover, we read in the Acts that St. Paul, after leaving Barnabas, found at Lystra Timothy, born of a Christian mother and already a disciple.[8] Clearly he was already baptized.

St. Paul, then, as the Acts relate, taking with him Timothy, circumcised him on account of the Jews, and for some time employed him as a helper that he might get to know his character. He wished himself to do what he enjoined upon others. ' Impose not hands lightly upon any man '[9] he was to say to Timothy when later on he was a bishop, referring, of course, to ordination, not to baptism, for that used to be administered forthwith. A similar precept did St. Paul give in regard to deacons, that they should be tested before they ministered. For some time, then, he kept Timothy with him as an assistant that he might make trial of him. But when he had been proved worthy he was ordained bishop by the imposition of St. Paul's hands, placed in authority over a church and given power to consecrate others. For to him was the command given : ' Impose not hands lightly upon any man.'

Similarly St. Paul made Titus a bishop, and set him over the Cretans with authority to consecrate others whom he might judge worthy. ' For this cause,' he writes, ' I left thee in Crete, that thou shouldest set in order the things that are wanting and shouldest ordain priests in every city, as I also appointed thee.'[10] Clearly Titus was to ordain by the same rite of imposition of hands as that by which St. Paul had ordained him. It was the same rite as that by which Saul and Barnabas had been separated for the apostolate, including the ceremonies of prayer, fasting and laying-on of hands. The same, too, as Paul and Barnabas employed, as we read in the fourteenth chapter of the Acts: 'And when they had ordained for them priests in every church, and had prayed with fasting, they commended them to the Lord.'[11]

The word χειροτονήσαντες is indeed used by the Greek writers of the people who elected their magistrates by raising their hands. But here St. Luke uses it in another sense. For he is not here speaking of the people, who indeed manifest their consent by lifting up their hands, but of the apostles, who by laying-on their hands ordained priests and placed them in authority over the people. Thus St. Jerome, commenting on the fifty-eighth chapter of Isaias, says that by χειροτονίαν is to be understood the ordination of clerics, which is performed not simply by prayer, but by the imposition of hands.[12]

Though it is related that the deacons also were ordained by the laying-on of hands, and therefore received a certain grace, yet we may be sure that as these ranks are different, so priests and deacons receive grace in varying degrees to help them to perform their different functions. The apostles laid hands on the deacons, as we read in the sixth chapter of the Acts, that they might receive a grace proportionate to their office. They commanded the brethren to look out among themselves for seven men of good reputation whom they might appoint to the office. To the brethren was the selection committed, since they knew the behaviour of others better than the apostles. But it was the apostles who by imposition of hands conferred upon them the office itself of the deacon. ' These they placed in the presence of the apostles: and they, praying, imposed hands upon them.'[13] But the apostles would never have imposed hands upon them had they not been taught by the Holy Ghost that grace would be thereby given. In some of them we can see how in actual fact grace did follow. Thus of Stephen it is said that he was full of grace and fortitude,[14] and of Philip we read that by his preaching, his signs and miracles he converted the Samaritans to Christ.[15]

Surely now it must be abundantly evident that by this outward sign, viz. the imposition of hands, grace is bestowed upon those who are duly ordained by the prelates of the Church to the pastoral office.

Section 13

TENTH AXIOM

Those who are lawfully ordained pastors and priests of the Church are called, and truly are, priests of God.

ISAIAS writes: 'You shall be called the priests of the Lord: to you it shall be said: Ye ministers of our God: you shall eat the riches of the Gentiles and you shall pride yourselves in their glory.'[1] These words refer to the apostles and their successors and foretell that they shall be called princes of the Church, priests of the Lord and ministers of God. In this sense do all writers interpret the passage who have ever yet dealt with it, nor can it be twisted to any other meaning except by violence.

Thus St. Jerome in his commentary on Isaias says of this passage: 'The builders of the cities that have been laid waste, the shepherds of the flocks, the husbandmen and dressers of the vine, the sons of strangers, all these are the priests of God to whom the prophet now says: You shall be called the priests of the Lord: to you it shall be said: Ye ministers of our God. He means, of course, the princes of the Church.'[2]

St. Clement, too, in his Epistle to James, where

§ 13]   SECOND REJOINDER   65

he speaks about priests and bishops, quotes the same words, thus: 'By the prophet He speaks, saying: You shall be called the priests of the Lord: to you it shall be said: Ye ministers of our God: you shall eat the riches of the Gentiles and you shall pride yourselves in their glory.'[3] The words certainly are applicable to the apostles and their successors. They 'ate the riches of the Gentiles,' for they converted the greatest of them to the faith and incorporated them with Christ. Thus it was said to Peter in regard to the Gentiles: 'Kill and eat.'[4] And they made contemptible the glory of the Gentiles when the Gentiles, with all the wisdom and eloquence of which they were so proud, were unable to withstand the apostles. Now neither the Gentiles nor the unbelieving Jews would refer to the apostles and their successors as ministers of our God, because they were not willing to acknowledge God as common to them and the Christians, but Christians will ever give them that title. Clearly, then, this prophecy proves that the pastors of the Church should be called priests of God.

But we shall prove the same from the New Testament. To begin with, Luther cannot deny that Christ Himself is called a priest according to the order of Melchisedech. David announces it in prophecy: 'The Lord hath sworn, and He will not repent: Thou art a priest for ever according to the order of Melchisedech.'[5] St. Paul quotes these words in the Epistle to the Hebrews to show that Christ is a priest according to the order of Melchisedech,[6] but not according to the order of Aaron. If this is so, Christ must have used in His sacrifice the same substances in which of old

Melchisedech offered sacrifice. Now the book of Genesis tells us that he sacrificed in bread and wine: 'Melchisedech the king of Salem brought forth bread and wine, for he was the priest of the most high God.'[7] Christ, therefore, was to sacrifice in bread and wine, but never did he do so except at the Last Supper, when under the appearance of bread and wine He instituted the sacrament of His body and blood. It follows that He offered sacrifice at the Last Supper. So necessary is this conclusion that I trust that no one, however impious or foolish, will deny it. If Christ was a priest according to the order of Melchisedech who sacrificed in bread and wine He Himself must have sacrificed in bread and wine, which He is nowhere read to have done except in the Cenacle.

But perhaps Luther will deny that Melchisedech's sacrifice was in bread and wine. For however certain and well established a thing may be these heretics are bold and impudent enough to deny it if it is in opposition to their tenets. But this fact is as certain as anything can well be. For immediately after the words 'Melchisedech brought forth bread and wine' it is added, 'for he was the priest of the most high God.' Why should these words be given as the cause of what goes before, unless it be to show that Melchisedech used bread and wine in his sacrifice?

Here Luther will exclaim that the phrase is wrongly translated from the Hebrew והוא כהן לאל עליון which means 'And he was the priest of the most high God,' as indeed St. Jerome translated it elsewhere.

But grant that it may be so rendered, it tells

equally in our favour, in so far as immediately after the mention of bread and wine it is added that he was the priest of the most high God. I would ask Luther to tell me what other kind of sacrifice Melchisedech ever offered. If he was a priest of some special order he must have offered some special sacrifice. As here, then, mention is made of bread and wine, which Christ also used when He instituted the sacrament of His body, and as no other kind of sacrifice is ever said in the Scriptures to have been offered by Melchisedech, how can anyone be so shameless as to deny that he ever offered sacrifice in these things?

Luther certainly would have an argument of some weight if nowhere else in Holy Scripture there were any mention of a sacrifice in bread and wine. For as Christ more than once is asserted to have been a priest according to the order of Melchisedech, it is of importance that there should be mention of some sacrifice common to them both. But as there is nowhere any mention of another sacrifice common to them it follows that this sacrifice in bread and wine is the one.

Though in this way our thesis is abundantly proved, yet we shall not shrink from the labour of quoting the testimony of the most learned writers, not only Latin and Greek, but Jewish also, that if possible Luther may be ashamed of his rashness in so far as he quotes for his heresy neither reason nor Scripture nor the testimony of any learned writer. Our purpose, then, is to make it abundantly clear that Melchisedech used to offer sacrifice in bread and wine. First we will speak of Latin writers.

St. Jerome, the most learned of Scriptural scholars, in his letter to Evagrius,[8] writes as follows: 'Melchisedech, because he was of Chanaan and not of the race of the Jews, was a type of the priesthood of the Son of God, of which it is written in the one hundred and ninth Psalm: "Thou art a priest for ever according to the order of Melchisedech." This order is interpreted in various ways, viz. because he alone was both king and priest and exercised his priesthood before the covenant of circumcision, so that the Jews received their priesthood after the Gentiles, not the Gentiles from the Jews; nor was he anointed with oil as the law of Moses commanded, but with the oil of gladness and purity of faith; nor did he offer victims of flesh and blood, nor receive the blood nor entrails of brute animals (i.e. anything above and beyond food),[9] but with simple bread and wine, and with a pure sacrifice he dedicated the sacrament of Christ.'

St. Augustine agrees, saying: 'In the priest Melchisedech we see our Lord's sacrifice prefigured, as Holy Scripture testifies: "And Melchisedech the King of Salem brought forth bread and wine. For he was the priest of the most high God and he blessed Abraham." And that Melchisedech was a type of Christ the Holy Ghost declares in the Psalm, saying in the person of the Father to the Son, "Before the day-star I begot Thee: Thou art a priest for ever according to the order of Melchisedech."'[10]

We may add St. Cyprian, who writes thus:[11] 'So that in the book of Genesis Abraham's blessing by the priest Melchisedech may be duly emphasized, his typical sacrifice in bread and wine is first mentioned. This type our Lord afterwards completed and fulfilled when He offered bread and wine mingled with water. He, who is the reality, fulfilled the truth of the shadow. So, too, by the mouth of Solomon[12] the Holy Ghost shows beforehand a type of the bread and wine, offered in sacrifice by our Lord, referring also to the altar and to the apostles. 'Wisdom hath built herself a house, she hath hewn her out seven pillars. She hath slain her victims, mingled her wine and set forth her table. She hath sent out her servants to invite with loud proclamation[13] to the cup, saying: "Whosoever is foolish, let him come to me." And to the unwise she said: "Come, eat my bread, and drink the wine which I have mingled for you."'

St. Ambrose agrees with the preceding: 'There was given to thee long before a type of these sacraments. It was in the time of Abraham, when he gathered together three hundred and eighteen servants, pursued his enemies and delivered his nephew. As he returned a victor he was met by the priest Melchisedech who offered him bread and wine. Who had bread and wine? Not Abraham but Melchisedech. Melchisedech, therefore, is the author of the sacraments.'[14]

Arnobius similarly writes: 'He who by the mystery of bread and wine was made a priest for ever according to the order of Melchisedech—Melchisedech who alone amongst priests offered bread and wine, when Abraham was returning victorious from the fight.'[15]

But let us turn to the Greeks. St. Chrysostom,

commenting on this passage, says: 'See how in the honour offered to the patriarch the sacrament is prefigured, for he offered him bread and wine. Having seen the type, look now to the fulfilment and admire the truth of the Scriptures. In earlier centuries, nay, even from the beginning, the future was foretold.'[16]

St. John Damascene is in complete agreement. 'As Abraham returned from the slaughter of the strangers he was received with gifts of bread and wine by Melchisedech who was a priest of the most high God. That banquet prefigured this mystical banquet, as that priest prefigured and shadowed forth the true priest Christ: "Thou art a priest for ever according to the order of Melchisedech."'[17]

Vulgarius, lastly, is in entire agreement. Writing on the Epistle to the Hebrews, he says: 'But to what other priest after the manner of Melchisedech can the Jews point but to Christ? Were not all others under the Law? Did they not all observe the sabbaths and offer the sacrifices of the Law? Clearly, then, what is said refers to Christ. For He, and He alone, after the manner of Melchisedech, sacrificed in bread and wine.'

What need to quote more authors? They all assert, as you see, dear reader, both these facts, viz. that both Melchisedech and Christ offered sacrifice in bread and wine. And as even the Jewish Rabbis assert it of Melchisedech, and bear witness that their Messias, when he comes, will do the same, what further room can there be for doubt?

So the Rabbi Semuel, according to the testimony of the Rabbi Moses Hadarsan, interpreting this passage of Genesis, said: 'Here the writer deals with the mysteries of the priesthood. For Melchisedech was sacrificing bread and wine to God who is holy and blessed, as it is said in the same place: "And he was a priest of the most high God."'

Rabbi Pinhas, the son of Jair, spoke thus: 'When the Messias comes all sacrifices shall cease, but the sacrifice of bread and wine shall never cease. As it is written in Genesis: "And Melchisedech King of Salem took bread and wine." Melchisedech stands for the Messias, the King who is to come. "Melchi" signifies King, for He is the King of the whole world. "Sedech" signifies justice. And He shall send forth His justice and peace over the whole world.' He added: 'The King of Salem, that is of the heavenly Jerusalem, took bread and wine, that is, when other sacrifices fail He will continue the sacrifice of bread and wine, as it is written in the one hundred and ninth Psalm: "Thou art a priest for ever according to the order of Melchisedech."'

The Rabbi Johai, who lived long before Christ, proves that the sacrifice of bread and wine will never cease, partly from the words of the Book of Judges: 'Can I forsake my wine that cheereth God and men?'[18] He says: 'Wine cheers men, but how does it cheer God?' His answer is: 'In the sacrifice which is made of wine.' He proves it, too, partly from the book of Psalms. For he adds: 'That the sacrifice of bread will never cease is clear from the seventy-first Psalm: "There shall be a cake of corn upon the earth, high up upon the hills."'[19]

In addition, many Jewish doctors, especially Rabbi Kimhi and Rabbi Selemon, interpret this Psalm absolutely of the Messias, and assert that his sacrifice will be in a cake of corn. The Chaldaic translation agrees, thus: 'There will be Corban, i.e. a sacrifice of corn on the earth, upon the high mountains of the Church.' In which words is clearly signified the manner of sacrificing which the priests now observe, i.e. the elevation of the host. For 'the mountains of the Church' most fitly expresses the priests and prelates of the Church.

If we have been tedious in these many quotations it is that there may remain no particle of doubt that as Melchisedech sacrificed in bread and wine, so Christ, who was a priest after his order, used the same substances in His sacrifice. And since so many important writers, Latin, Greek and Jewish, agree on this point; and Scripture, far from opposing it, gives it the strongest support, nor ever ascribes to Melchisedech any other priesthood save the sacrifice of bread and wine, who now will have any further hesitation in asserting that Christ and Melchisedech offered sacrifice by means of the same substances?

But as not only in the early days of the Church's history, but throughout the whole of its course (as we have shown in the fifth axiom), priests were necessary, it follows that the successors of the apostles were also priests and had the power to offer sacrifice. 'Do this in commemoration of Me'[20] was a command not only for the apostles, but for all those who with similar authority should succeed them in the rule of the Church. So, then, dear reader, not only do we see in the Old Testament, from the prophecy of Isaias, that the pastors of the Christian flock are called priests of the Lord, but we find in the New Testament the reason why they should be so called.

Section 14

CONCLUSION OF SECOND REJOINDER

WE have now built up our ten axioms for the second rejoinder to Luther.

The first shows that for six undeniable reasons there must be placed over the multitude men to care for its interests.

The second, that in fact Christ appointed such men to feed, govern and teach His, i.e. the Christian, flock.

The third, that such men need a more abundant grace that they may the better discharge their office.

The fourth, that in fact Christ did bestow such grace upon the pastors He appointed.

The fifth, that these offices must necessarily be continued in the Church until the Last Day.

The sixth, that no one lawfully discharges such an office unless he be duly called, ordained and sent.

The seventh, that those who are legitimately appointed to such offices are undoubtedly to be believed to be called by the Holy Ghost.

The eighth, that at the moment when they are thus appointed they receive always the grace of the same Spirit unless they place a hindrance in the way.

§ 14]   SECOND REJOINDER   75

The ninth, that the Holy Spirit infallibly gives this grace at the performance of some external rite, i.e. the imposition of hands.

The tenth, that the pastors and priests, so ordained by the imposition of hands, are truly priests of God and offer sacrifice both for themselves and for their flock.

From these axioms, which we have fully established from the Holy Scriptures, it is clearly proved that in the Church there are some functions, instituted by Christ and His Holy Spirit, which are not common to each and every one of the people. For not all are called to the office of feeding, teaching and ruling the flock. But without call and ordination (as we have shown) no one may usurp these functions. We do not deny, however, that all the people are called priests in Holy Scripture, but their priesthood, in comparison with the other, is metaphorical. For the people in the same sense in which they are called priests are also, as we shall show, called kings. Each one as a king rules himself and in like manner is a priest to himself alone.

All Christians, then, are kings and priests, but to themselves, not to others. But the pastors and priests of whom we speak are priests for the whole flock in the sense that they feed and rule them. For they are mediators between Christ and the people that they may teach the people what they have learnt from Christ or His Spirit. For this reason does St. Peter, as we have seen, call Christ the Prince of Pastors. For as they feed the flock they are in turn fed by Christ.

Moreover, the priests of whom we speak have to render an account for the souls of their subjects, but the people have not in turn to render an account for the souls of their priests. Again, priests, although they are 'taken from among men,' are yet 'appointed for men in the things that appertain to God.'[1] But the people, on the other hand, are not appointed to act as intermediaries to God for their priests. Priests, therefore, being of the same flesh and blood as the people, are to offer sacrifice continually both for themselves and for the sins of the people.

Thus the victim by which chiefly they are to appease the anger of God is the sacrifice of the altar in which under the appearance of bread and wine according to the order of Melchisedech they offer continually the body and blood of Christ. Luther with a great show of words boasted arrogantly that he had proved no priest nor mediator to be necessary to the people except Christ. It will now be clear, I trust, how utterly unfounded is this assertion. So may we say, too, of his assertions that every Christian is a sufficient priest to himself to teach himself and to perform all the other priestly functions, and that all other offices that are not common to the whole people have been set up by the lies of men and the deceits of Satan. For from the foregoing axioms it will be obvious to all that the office of these men, whom for the moment we may call go-betweens or mediators between Christ and the flock, was not established by any human invention, but by the divine institution of Christ and the Holy Spirit.

Section 15

THIRD REJOINDER

Introduction

IT remains now to make our third rejoinder to Luther and to show that he can quote nothing, whether from the Holy Scriptures or from the writings of orthodox teachers, in support of his heresy. We will take the texts of Scripture as he has arranged them and refute them one by one.

Attempting to show that the one and only priesthood for us is that of Christ, whereby He offered Himself for us and all of us with Himself, he quotes St. Peter's words: 'Christ died once for our sins, the just for the unjust, that He might offer us to God, being put to death, indeed, in the flesh, but brought to life by the Spirit.'[1]

We reply that there is no obscurity in these words. For the reason why Christ offered Himself to the Father as a victim for our sins, the just for the unjust, was not that He had offered us as a victim again and again, for we were not yet in being, but that in the future, when we should have shown ourselves obedient to His laws, He might present us, truly justified, to His Father. That will surely come to pass if we keep ourselves pure and undefiled from the evil desires of a former sinful life. But this in no way hinders our being meanwhile fed, ruled and taught by priests. Indeed, through their care and solicitude for us we shall far more easily and surely be preserved pure and undefiled.

He quotes, too, the words of St. Paul to the Hebrews: 'By one oblation He hath perfected for ever them that are sanctified.'[2]

I do not suppose that Luther concludes from these words that every Christian, however great a sinner he has been, is yet sanctified by this oblation once made. For it is certain that innumerable Christians will be condemned to eternal punishment. Only those, then, are certainly sanctified by this oblation to whom its merits are communicated by the sacraments of the Church. For clearly he who refuses to be baptized when he has the opportunity will never share in the benefit of Christ's oblation. As, then, Baptism is one means by which we receive the virtue of that oblation, so the Sacrament of the Altar is another, which as often as it is celebrated shows forth to us the oblation once made upon the Cross. Although, therefore, one victim was long ago offered by Christ and was sufficient as a propitiation to the Father for innumerable sins, yet the same sacrifice is renewed as often as the mystery of the body and blood of Christ is celebrated upon the altar. We have already written at great length upon the subject in the book in which on behalf of our most illustrious king we answered Luther's curses,[3] and we shall treat of it again a little later. For since we all sin daily, and now indeed far more gravely after the one oblation of Christ, a victim is now no less necessary than before, since now our sins are far more grave. Although then Christ does not die for us a second time, yet in order that the merits of the death that He once suffered for us be applied to us again when we have sinned, the sacrifice of the altar must be frequently renewed. This is done by those whom before we called go-betweens or mediators between Christ and the people. From these texts, therefore, no one can rightly infer that there need be no priests as intermediaries between Christ and the people.

Luther, then, from these texts tries to deduce that the priesthood of Christ is spiritual and is common to all Christians. 'We are all,' he says, 'sharers in the priesthood of Christ, all of us who are Christians, i.e. children of Christ the high priest.'

We reply that though it is not a just inference from these particular texts yet what he says is true. But not every one of the people is a priest in the sense in which Christ is one. For many things are asserted of Him which cannot be applied to individual Christians in the same manner in which they are attributed to Him. We agree, however, that in one sense Luther's words are true, in the sense, that is to say, that every Christian is a priest to himself, as we have said. But besides this priesthood which is common to all, it is evident from what we have said that there must be a special priesthood exercised by those who by the rulers of the Church are lawfully called, ordained and sent, who are priests not to themselves alone, but to the people over whom by their lawful vocation they are placed.

Luther continues: 'Nor do we need any other priest or mediator except Christ, for every priest is chosen, as the apostle says, that he may pray for the people and teach them. But every Christian by himself prays in Christ, having by Him, as St. Paul says, access to God. So did Isaias promise: "And it shall come to pass that before they call I will hear; as they are yet speaking, I will hear."[4] Thus they are taught by themselves from God, according to the same prophet: "I will make all thy children to be taught of the Lord."[5] So, too, Jeremias: "They shall teach no more every man his neighbour, and every man his brother, saying: Know the Lord. For all shall know Me from the least of them even to the greatest."[6] Isaias again says: "The earth is filled with the knowledge of the Lord as the covering waters of the sea."[7] Hence Christ calls the people θεοδιδάκτους, "It is written in the prophets: And they shall all be taught of God."[8] From these texts Luther thinks and asserts that every visible priesthood is abolished, for the two chief offices of the priest, praying and teaching, are now, as he boasts, proved to be common to all Christians.

I reply that these texts of Scripture are as infallibly true as the earlier ones Luther has quoted, but that he is deceiving his followers through a false interpretation of them. For if there were no pastor needful to the Christian people beyond Christ, then it was idle for Christ to adjure Peter, if he loved Him, to feed His sheep.[9] This Christ did in solemn manner, repeating His adjuration three times. But what need was there for Peter to feed the sheep of Christ if they needed no teacher except Christ? Equally vain was it for St. Peter to exhort the priests to 'feed the flock of God,' promising that 'when the Prince of Pastors should appear they should receive a never-fading crown of glory.'[10] Clearly, then, Christ must have under Him other pastors whose duty it is to feed His flock, otherwise St. Peter would not call Him the Prince of Pastors.

Vainly, too, if Luther is right, did St. Paul so solemnly charge Timothy. 'I charge thee before God and Jesus Christ who shall judge the living and the dead, by His coming, preach the word; be instant in season, reprove, rebuke, exhort with all mildness and learning.'[11] Nor need he have so earnestly admonished Titus to hold fast 'that faithful word that is according to doctrine, that he might be able to exhort in sound doctrine and convince the gainsayers.'[12]

From such words no one can fail to see that pastors are necessary in the Church of God to watch diligently over the instruction of the Christian flock. Therefore the texts that Luther quotes are to be understood partly of the early days of the Church's history when the Holy Ghost descended visibly upon individual Christians and all were taught by the same Spirit; partly of the future state of glory, and this is the more common interpretation, when, every veil being drawn aside, all shall be openly taught by God Himself. But meanwhile whilst, as St. Paul says, 'we are absent from the Lord,'[13] each congregation needs to have its pastor to teach and to rule, by word and example, the flock committed to him.

Of course, I do not deny that all the efforts of the external teacher are in vain unless the Holy Spirit inwardly illuminates the heart. But although for the apostles and supreme rulers of the Church this illumination may have been abundant, and fully sufficient without any other teacher, yet it is not in the same measure given to all, but for the vast majority of men is so dim as to be totally insufficient without the help of another teacher. This I think has been made so clear by what I have said above that it is needless to adduce further witnesses in proof. But that we may see still more evidently that Luther can derive no support from the texts he has quoted, we will deal with them one by one.

Section 16

FIRST TEXT

' By Christ we have access to God.'[1]

WE reply. St. Paul did not precisely say this, but rather: ' By Christ we have access through faith into this glory wherein we stand.' St. Paul does not here try to show that each Christian has access to God, but that through the faith of Christ we reach the grace in which we stand, which of course is most true. Not that we deny that each Christian can by himself pray to God, though St. Paul's words do not here deal with that point. But from our admission let no one jump to the conclusion that no other intercessor is necessary. For if anyone need have had no fear to approach God by himself, it was surely St. Paul, and yet more than once he considers the prayers of others needful for him. Thus he writes : ' I beseech you, therefore, brethren, through our Lord Jesus Christ and by the charity of the Holy Ghost, that you assist me in your prayers for me to God.'[2] And again : ' You helping withal in prayer for us, that, for this gift obtained for us by many persons, thanks may be given by many in our behalf.'[3] And again : ' Praying withal for us also, that God may open to us a door of speech, to speak the mystery of Christ.'⁴ Once more: 'Watching with all instance and supplication for all the saints, and for me, that speech may be given me, that I may open my mouth with confidence, to make known the mystery of the Gospel.'⁵ If, then, St. Paul, who was filled with the Holy Ghost, tells us that he requires the prayers of others, how much more do others who have not yet obtained equal grace with St. Paul stand in need of intercessors. To take another point, unless we needed the prayers of others it would have been idle for St. James to urge the Christians, whenever one of them was sick, to call in the priests of the Church to pray for him. But we are labouring to prove the obvious.

Section 17

SECOND TEXT

'*And it shall come to pass that before they call I will hear ; as they are yet speaking, I will hear.*'[1]

WE reply. Many of the things, if not all, that are read in that chapter cannot be otherwise interpreted than of the state of eternal happiness, as for example the words that occur a little earlier : 'Behold I create Jerusalem a rejoicing, and the people thereof joy. And I will rejoice in Jerusalem and joy in My people. And the voice of weeping shall no more be heard in her, nor the voice of crying. There shall no more be an infant of days there, nor an old man that shall not fill up his days.'[2] Obviously such words cannot be understood of any earthly Jerusalem.

But even if we grant that the text in question is to be understood of this earth, it yet does not follow from it that we need no intercessor beyond Christ. For if now, during our earthly pilgrimage, each one's prayer is so sufficient to him that he needs no other mediator, but each Christian before he calls is heard, then it was idle for St. Paul to make such constant mention of the Romans 'always in his prayers, beseeching that by any means he might at length have a prosperous journey by the will of God in coming to them.'³ In vain did he pray always for the Thessalonians that God would make them worthy of His calling.⁴ In vain did he desire of Timothy ' first of all that supplications, prayers, intercessions and thanksgivings be made for all men, for kings and for all who are in high stations, that we may lead a quiet and peaceful life.'⁵ In vain did he of the same Timothy make remembrance without ceasing in his prayers night and day.⁶

Clearly, then, the prayers of others *can* help us, nor is a man's own prayer always enough, nor is everyone always heard before he prays to God. And just as all can be helped by the prayers of others, so can they be taught also by others, although Luther holds that each one immediately is taught by God.

As we have said above, we are ready to accept this tenet of Luther's if it is rightly understood, for certainly the efforts of an external teacher will be in vain unless the heart be internally enlightened by God. But this enlightenment is not given in equal measure to all, and in many is so faint that without some other teacher it is not always very profitable. But let us now listen to the texts by which Luther seeks to prove that no Christian needs any other teacher but himself.

Section 18

THIRD TEXT

' I will make all thy children to be taught of the Lord.'[1]

IT is certain that from this fifty-fourth chapter of Isaias, and also from the sixty-fifth, of which we have already spoken, the Jews conceived their error that a thousand years were to be spent with Christ upon this earth in the enjoyment of all sorts of carnal pleasure. Though a few Christians, and in particular Lactantius, seem to have favoured this error, yet notoriously it was rejected by the vast majority. There are, indeed, in either chapter, passages which can in no wise be applied to the present life. Thus: ' The voice of weeping shall no more be heard in her, nor the voice of crying. There shall no more be an infant of days there, nor an old man who shall not fill up his days.'[2] These words will never be fulfilled except in the future life. Again: ' This thing is to me as in the days of Noe, to whom I swore that I would no more bring in the waters of the deluge upon the earth: so have I sworn not to be angry with thee, and not to rebuke thee.'[3] As referring to this life, these words are unintelligible, for now there is no one who does not sin, nor one with whom, when he sins deliberately, God is not angry. Or again: 'Behold I will lay thy stones in order, and will lay thy foundations with sapphires, and I will make thy bulwarks of jasper, and thy gates of graven stones, and all thy borders of desirable stones.'[4] This corresponds rather with the vision given to St. John of the heavenly Jerusalem whose foundations he describes as adorned with every kind of precious stone: 'The first foundation jasper, the second sapphire, the third a chalcedony, the fourth an emerald, the fifth sardonyx, the seventh sardius, the eighth beryl, the ninth a topaz, the tenth a chrysoprasus, the eleventh a jacinth, the twelfth an amethyst.'[5]

Clearly, then, these two chapters of Isaias are to be understood of the state of future glory, i.e. when 'God shall wipe away all tears from their eyes, and death shall be no more, nor mourning, nor crying, nor sorrow shall be any more,'[6] as it is expressed in the same chapter. Then truly there will no more be heard the voice of weeping, nor the voice of crying; nor will there be more an infant of days, nor an old man who does not fill up his days. No one will sin, nor will God be angry with any, nor threaten any. There shall be nothing unclean, but the whole city shall shine and be glorious on all sides, as with precious stones. Nor, finally, will there be need of any other teacher except God, in whom the blessed shall see all things. Wherefore, then, all the children of the Church shall be taught by the Lord, and great shall be the peace of her children, and they shall be founded in justice.[7]

Very far is this from the condition of many who truly believe and live as members of the Church

Militant. For though there may be some who are taught by the Lord, who enjoy a great peace and who are confirmed in justice, yet obviously not all are in this condition. For very many who have faith, and thus even in Luther's opinion are members of the Church, do not enjoy a great peace nor are established in justice, for they frequently fall away from both.

Section 19

FOURTH TEXT

'They shall teach no more every man his neighbour, and every man his brother, saying: Know the Lord. For all shall know Me from the least of them even to the greatest.'[1]

NOW although these words had a partial fulfilment when the Holy Ghost came down upon the disciples gathered together on the day of Pentecost, yet they will not have a complete and perfect fulfilment except in the state of future glory. For not only do they foretell that no man shall any more be taught by his neighbour, but they go on thus: 'I will remember their sin no more.' But who doubts that of the many who have received the faith the great majority shall suffer punishment for their sins? How, then, shall it be that after the giving of the New Law God will be no more mindful of sin? And, again, if in literal truth no one was henceforth to teach his neighbour, surely neither Christ upon St. Peter, nor SS. Peter and Paul upon others, would have so earnestly inculcated the duty of teaching their neighbours.

I foresee Luther's objection. He will say that in the Epistle to the Hebrews St. Paul quotes the words as applicable to the present condition of the Church.² I admit the fact, but it does not necessarily follow that they have now, in the present time, their complete fulfilment. The promulgation of the Old Law and its reward were not contemporaneous, although the Old Testament embraced both, for the Law was promulgated on Mount Sinai, while the reward was in the promised land. Similarly, the New Testament includes a New Law and a reward for its observance, but while the one was promulgated on Mount Sion,³ the other we hope for in heaven. Thus both Isaias and St. Paul, as they spoke of the law which was to be written upon the hearts of men, added something about the reward for keeping that law, not, however, assigning both to the same time.

St. Augustine expounds the matter in his book *On the Spirit and the Letter*,⁴ saying : ' As the law of works, written on tables of stone, and its reward, the land of promise which the carnal house of Israel received when it was delivered from Egypt, both appertained to the Old Testament ; so the law of faith, written in men's hearts, and its reward, the vision of God, which the spiritual house of Israel will receive when it shall be delivered from this world, both appertain to the New Testament.' Of the two things, then, contained under the New Testament, the one, the writing of the law upon men's hearts, belongs to a time different from the other, the bestowal of the reward. Therefore St. Augustine immediately adds : ' Then shall be fulfilled the words of the apostle,' whether prophecies shall be made void, or tongues shall cease, or knowledge shall be destroyed.'⁵ That is to say the knowledge, as of children, in which we pass this life, the knowledge by which we now see through a glass in a dark manner, the knowledge which needs to be supplemented by prophecy, since now there is a succession of past and future, the knowledge to aid which are given tongues, i.e. a multiplicity of lessons, for he needs to be taught one thing in one manner, another in another, who is not yet admitted with purified mind to the contemplation of the eternal light of perfect truth.

'When, however, that which is perfect shall come, and that which is in part shall be done away, then He, who took our flesh that He might be seen by men, shall show Himself to them that love Him. Then it shall be eternal life to know the one true God,[6] then we shall be like to Him,[7] for we shall then know even as we are known.[8] Then shall not every man teach his fellow-citizen or his brother, saying, "Know the Lord," for all shall know Him, from the least of them even to the greatest.' From these words of St. Augustine it is clear that the words of Jeremias cannot be understood as referring to the individual members of the Church Militant.

But though we grant to Luther that every Christian knows the Lord, yet do we not daily see that those who have the faith of God yet need to be taught other things? Did not the Hebrews have the faith of God, to whom St. Paul said: 'You have need to be taught again what are the first rudiments of the word of God?'[9] Or the Galatians, whom when they were overtaken by any fault, he wished to be instructed by those who were spiritual?[10] Or the thousands of Jews of whose faith in Christ we read in the Acts of the Apostles, did not they need another teacher when they were at the same time zealous followers of the Law, and thought circumcision necessary for salvation? If, then, the Jews who had visibly received the Holy Ghost were nevertheless imbued with this error, and therefore in need of a teacher, what shall we say of the multitude of present-day Christians? Do not they too need teachers?

Section 20

FIFTH TEXT

'The earth is filled with the knowledge of the Lord as the covering waters of the sea.'[1]

WE reply that this prophecy was fulfilled in the time of the apostles when they were in a visible manner filled with the Holy Ghost and when ' their sound went forth to the whole earth.'[2] For then the whole world was filled with the knowledge of the Lord, as the earth is covered with the waters of the sea. But it by no means follows that since then there has been no need of any teacher; indeed, the very opposite is obviously the case.

Section 21

SIXTH TEXT

From the Gospel of St. John, where our Lord calls the people θεοδιδάκτους : *And it is written in the prophets : And they shall all be taught of God.*'[1]

WE reply that no one believes without the gift of faith, for St. Paul says : 'It is the gift of God, and not of yourselves.'[2] But to be inspired by faith is, in our Lord's teaching, the same as being taught by God. Wherefore we do not deny that everyone who believes in Christ is taught by God. But this inner action of God is for the most part so imperceptible, even to him who receives it, that undoubtedly he needs some other teacher.

Here, perhaps, Luther will try to snatch an advantage against us, because these very words are written in that chapter of Isaias which, as we have argued above, does not refer to the present state of the Church. But his attack fails. Christ says not that He took the words from Isaias, but from the prophets. It may be that they are written in other books of the prophets which have perished. It is not necessary that we should always be able to produce the books from which in the Scriptures quotations are taken. For example, in the Acts of the Apostles, St. Paul quotes some words of Christ which are nowhere found in the Gospels. He speaks of 'the word of the Lord Jesus, how He said: It is more blessed to give than to receive.'[3] But this is nowhere read in the Gospels. And in the Gospels themselves there are some quotations which are not to be found in any of the extant books of the Old Testament.

Section 22

CONCLUSION TO REFUTATION OF FIRST ATTACK

FROM what we have said it is clear how far Luther strays from the truth when he maintains that these texts have disproved our priesthood. For so does he continue after quoting the texts we have considered. ' These texts utterly disprove any visible priesthood, for they make common to all Christians access to God, prayer and teaching, which things are commonly regarded as peculiar to a priesthood. For what need is there of a priest when there is no need of a mediator or a teacher? Shall we have priests with no office to perform? But there is for Christians no other mediator or teacher than Christ.'

On the contrary, we have already shown that besides our Lord other teachers and mediators are required. We grant, indeed, that unless Christ teaches within, bestowing faith and giving some measure of light to the soul, vain will be the efforts of any teacher. But the Holy Spirit grants these gifts in such measure that they do not suffice in every individual soul to give a full knowledge of the Church's doctrine without the help of any other teacher. Christians may be imbued with faith, they may believe in God and pray to Him for help without any kind of intermediary, but obviously there will be many points which they will not understand without a teacher. Even though sometimes they might manage by themselves, yet they could not always do so without a helper. I cannot imagine how anyone, unless he be obstinately blind, can fail to see the necessity of someone to stand between Christ and His flock, not only to pray constantly and intercede with Christ for the people, but also to instruct the ignorant, to rouse those that slumber, to warn the careless and to carry out the other duties of pastors of souls. Thus, too, it is clear how false is what follows:

'Nay, even those who are not yet priests, that is not yet Christians, may of themselves approach to God and, taught by Him, may then be themselves mediators and teachers.'

We admit that every Christian may by himself draw near to God; he may say the Our Father, and beg for pardon and grace. But it is obvious that men who are not yet Christians are quite unfitted to teach others. And even though some could, yet all must see that the others would need intercessors and teachers to warn, stir up, teach and rebuke.

He continues: 'Therefore the priesthood of the New Testament dwells equally in all, by the Spirit alone, without any respect of persons. As the apostle says: "In Christ Jesus there is neither Jew nor Greek, there is neither bond nor free, there is neither male nor female, for you are all one in Christ Jesus." '[1]

THIRD REJOINDER

We reply. Though they be in one body, yet there is no reason why the members should not be various and endowed with different gifts. St. Paul says that within the unity of one body ' some He gave to be apostles, some prophets, some evangelists and others pastors and teachers.'[2] It is quite clear, too, that these names cannot be applied indiscriminately to every one of the people, for elsewhere the apostle writes that not all are apostles, nor all prophets, nor all doctors.[3] Luther's teaching, then, is, on this point at any rate, in the clearest and most direct opposition to the truth of the Scriptures.

' But let us continue,' says Luther (adding obscenities which we omit), ' to collect texts which establish the priesthood of the New Law, that we may silence the mouth of these impudent men. And first St. Peter's words : " Wherefore, laying aside all malice and all guile, and dissimulations and envies and all detractions, as new-born infants, desire the rational milk without guile, that thereby you may grow unto salvation : if yet you have tasted that the Lord is sweet. To whom approaching, the living stone, rejected indeed by men, but chosen and honoured of God, be you also, as living stones, built up a spiritual house, a holy priesthood, to offer up spiritual sacrifices, acceptable to God by Jesus Christ."[4] And further on : " But you are a chosen generation, a royal priesthood . . . that you may declare His virtues who hath called you out of darkness into His admirable light." Secondly, there is the witness of the Apocalypse : " Thou hast made us to our God a kingdom and priests."[5] Thirdly, also of the Apocalypse : " In these the second death hath no power, but they shall be priests of God and of Christ, and shall reign with Him a thousand years."[6]

'Now, although the Book of the Apocalypse, according to the reckoning of the ancient writers, is not of full authority in controversy, yet we have thought it well to take from it, for the confusion of our opponents, texts in which it is certain that all Christians are spoken of, and are called priests and kings; for just as they cannot be understood of visible kings, so neither, in the judgement of the whole Christian world, can they be understood of visible priests.'

Luther's last words clear away all ambiguity from the texts he has above quoted. Every one of the people is a priest in no other way than he is a king. But he is a king, not in such a way as to rule others. Therefore he is a priest, not for others, but for himself. But we are speaking of priests who by the prelates of the Church are called and ordained to this office, God co-operating and giving them grace from on high. These texts, therefore, are beside the purpose. Not that we deny that every Christian is a priest and a king, but he is so to himself and not to others. For just as it is not given to everyone to claim the rule over his fellows, so neither may he claim the mystery of the sacred rites. In brief, as everyone is a king, so is he a priest. But it is not lawful for everyone to rule over others. Therefore not everyone is a priest.

Luther goes on: 'But outside these three passages there is no other place in the New Testament where there is any mention by name of a priesthood.'

But, we reply, even if the Scriptures do not mention priests by their specific name, it does not therefore follow that there are no priests at all. We have often shown how illogical and unconvincing is this negative argument. Holy Scripture often mentions presbyters and bishops, and as they are in fact absolutely the same as those whom to-day we call priests, it is a pure sophistry to deny that there is any mention of priests, on the ground that nothing is said of them under this name, when there is constant mention of them under the name of presbyters and bishops.

We spoke above of the reason why the apostles generally avoided the use of the word, i.e. because the priests of the Old Law were still exercising their functions. Partly, then, that the priests of the Jews might not be irritated, partly to avoid confusion, the apostles are thought to have for a time avoided this name. But, whether it was for this reason or any other, it is certain that they are most frequently called by them bishops and presbyters.

'But,' someone may ask, 'why, then, do the apostles so often in the sacred books call all Christians priests?' I reply that when the Jewish priests understood that Christians were called by the apostles priests in no other way than they were called kings, they could have no reason for irritation. For they knew full well that to their own nation in almost the same words it had been said: 'For all the earth is mine, and you shall be to Me a priestly kingdom and a holy nation.'[7] The Jews knew well enough that these words were spoken of the whole people, but they were not therefore under the illusion that every individual was a king or a priest, otherwise they would not have accused Christ for calling Himself a king.

Luther proceeds : ' Before going further, let us here stop a moment to hurl a few gibes at the monsters and idols of this world, the Pope and his priests. Come now, you fine priests, show us one jot or tittle from the whole of the Gospels or Epistles to prove that you are, or ought to be, called in any special way priests, or that your order is a priesthood different from the general priesthood of all Christians. Why do you not reply ? Can you hear me, you deaf images ? Go to the schools of Paris, I beg you, where in place of texts of Scripture they issue their official decrees.[8] " This proposition is heretical and injurious to the sacerdotal order : let this decree be to you an article of faith." Where do you come from, you priests of idols ? Why have you stolen the name that is common to us all and appropriated it to yourselves ? You are guilty of sacrilege and blasphemy against the Universal Church, for you have violently snatched from others a holy title and now abuse it, turning it merely to tyranny, to ostentatious avarice and lust. Again I say : We regard you priests as the idols of the world. What can you say for yourselves, you intolerable burdens upon the whole world ? You are not priests and yet you call yourselves such. Think what you deserve, you notorious thieves and hypocrites.'

Surely no one who reads this will imagine that he is listening to a man of sane mind and Christian spirit, but rather to a mad dog spurred on by the furies of hell. But let him keep his abuse ; we will proceed with our argument. And although the axioms we have above established are quite a sufficient answer to this outburst of Luther's, yet we will add more.

First I would ask the reader to notice how unjustly Luther attacks the priests of the present day, for it is not true that they have usurped to themselves this name, nor imagined nor invented it now for the first time. For if any deserve to be attacked for this cause it is rather those whom we have quoted above: Origen, St. Basil, St. Athanasius, Eusebius, SS. Cyril, Chrysostom, Cyprian, Ambrose, Jerome and Augustine, who were so blind that far from detecting the error which now Luther proclaims, they embraced it as a most evident truth. Still more should Luther attack SS. Ignatius, Polycarp, Clement and Gregory Nazianzen, Dionysius, Hegesippus, Philo, Eusebius and other men of their age, who, being the contemporaries of the apostles themselves, should not have taught the Church anything beyond what they had learned from them. But most of all should Luther direct his insults to the Holy Ghost, who dwells in the Church, being sent for this very purpose, viz., that He may lead it into all truth.[9] Yet the Holy Ghost, from the very earliest days of the Church's history, allowed what Luther calls this pestilent error to establish itself and, with such great harm to souls, to be continued through so many centuries until the present day in every church of Christendom.

We cannot doubt that all the early Fathers of whom we have spoken were inspired by the Holy Ghost. If, then, Luther is inspired by the same Spirit he would hold no other opinion than theirs, especially as they are so unanimous in their teaching and their words. Much more just it would be to attack Luther, who despises the Fathers, and, though they are so numerous, so renowned for learning, so full of the Holy Ghost, follows the mad dreams of his own head. Priests, indeed, would deserve to be attacked if that name which, far from usurping to themselves, they have had handed down to them from so many learned and holy Fathers, they should now lay aside because of the mad ravings of a lunatic. To anyone who is not entirely malicious it is quite sufficient that in the New Testament, whether Luther likes it or not, a clear distinction is drawn between pastors and flock, i.e. between rulers and people, and that at duly conducted ordinations of pastors God infallibly assists, giving grace and approving what is done. For this, so far as the thing itself is concerned, is abundantly clear to all, however much Luther may cavil at the word. It must be clear, too, to all that this office is not a human invention, nor a deceit of Satan, but divinely instituted by the Holy Ghost.

Nor should anyone be disturbed by the fact that so rarely is the priesthood mentioned under its specific name. If he cares to make a detailed study of the various terms used by the writers of the New Testament he will find that they did not very exactly discriminate between them. They were not very precise in their use of words and handed down to the next generation many things by word of mouth which they did not put into writing. That this may be clear I will give some examples.

§ 22] THIRD REJOINDER 105

The words 'ministry' and 'minister' may seem to belong to all Christians and in this sense they are used more than once in the New Testament, but yet in a special sense they are applied to apostles, bishops and presbyters, and that very frequently. Thus to Timothy St. Paul writes: 'Fulfil thy ministry";[10] and to the Colossians: 'Say to Archippus: Take heed to the ministry which thou hast received in the Lord, that thou fulfil it.'[11] In the Acts we read of the election of Matthias 'to take the place of this ministry.'[12] In these passages there is undoubtedly question not of the general ministry which was common to all Christians, but of the special one that belonged exclusively to apostles, bishops and presbyters. This appears yet more clearly in the passage dealing with the prophets and doctors at Antioch. The old translation has: 'As they were ministering to the Lord and fasting'; but Erasmus renders it: 'As they were sacrificing to the Lord and fasting.'[13] For λειτουργία is a word used for those who minister by sacred rites, which belongs to priests alone. For this reason the sacrifice of the altar is often by the Fathers called the liturgy.

The word 'presbyter' in its original meaning is common to all who are advanced in age, as St. Paul uses it to Timothy: 'An ancient man rebuke not, but entreat him as a father; young men as brethren; old women as mothers.'[14] Here the Greek word used for 'ancient' is 'presbyter.' Yet the very same word has a different use even in the mouth of St. Paul himself. Thus he writes to Titus: 'For this cause I left thee in Crete, that thou shouldest ordain presbyters in every city.'[15]

Here certainly the word has reference not to age, but to dignity. Titus could confer a dignity, but not add to a man's age.

Note also that both Titus and Timothy were young men. St. Paul writes to the latter: 'Let no man despise thy youth.'[16] And yet both were presbyters.

So, too, the names of bishops and presbyters are often confused, and the same men called by both names. Thus we read that St. Paul sent messengers from Miletus to Ephesus and called together the presbyters of the church. When they came he addressed them at length, adding towards the end: 'Take heed to yourselves and to all the flock over which the Holy Ghost hath placed you bishops to rule the Church of God which He hath purchased with His own blood.'[17] Those same persons who a little before are called presbyters he now calls bishops, asserting that they are placed by the Holy Ghost to rule the Church of God. Certainly it is not a duty incumbent upon all Christians to rule the Church of God.

The term 'apostle,' again, in its literal sense is common also to the seventy disciples. Thus does St. John use the word when he says: 'The apostle is not greater than he that sent him.'[18] For 'apostle' means 'sent,' and the seventy also were sent, as St. Luke shows.[19] Yet the word in its special sense was applicable only to very few, as everybody knows.

We could add several other examples, but these will suffice to show that words of this kind are sometimes not clearly distinguished from one another in writing, but that for their more exact discrimination we must have recourse to oral tradition.

But if anyone argues from the purely negative ground that because the ministers were never called by the apostles by the technical term of 'priests,' therefore there were no priests, we would reply that we could as easily prove that St. John the Evangelist thought that there was no distinction between the apostles and the disciples. For throughout his whole Gospel he never once calls the apostles by their proper name. Of course, he is constantly speaking of them, but he calls them not apostles but disciples. Shall we, then, say that there was no distinction between apostles and disciples? It does not follow. Similarly when the writers of the New Testament make no mention of the specific term 'priests' it does not follow that there was no distinction between priests and the rest of the Christian body. For they speak constantly of them under other titles, viz. presbyters and bishops.

Nor need we be surprised if later on the Holy Ghost willed that there should be different ranks in the priesthood, since so clear an example of the same sort of thing is given us by Christ in the Gospel. It was not without a purpose that He instituted the rank of the twelve apostles as distinct from the seventy disciples, and then the rank of the seventy disciples as distinct from the rest of the people. And if Christ thought such a distinction of ranks necessary even for that 'little flock,'[20] surely it was far more necessary for the whole body of Christians who were soon to exceed in number the very stars of the heavens. We must believe, then, that it was most fitting, and in accordance with the guidance of the Holy Ghost, that to the apostles succeeded those whom we call bishops or greater priests insofar as they hold the first rank in the Church; to the seventy disciples, those whom we call presbyters or lesser priests, who hold the second rank. It was fitting that this distinction, instituted by Christ, should be perpetuated in the Church, that there might for ever be some who should represent the apostles, others the disciples. I suppose no heretic would be so impudent as to say that this distinction of rank was not instituted by Christ, but introduced later by the apostles. Consequently, then, he must agree that these ranks are not held by every individual Christian, but by those only who have been legitimately called and ordained to such office by the rulers of the Church.

What Luther goes on to assert upon this point is of no weight and undeserving of reply. Of this be certain, dear reader, that Luther can bring against the priesthood nothing but negative arguments, and such arguments weigh nothing with learned men. True it is that he quotes texts which seem to say that nothing must be added to the Scriptures, nor any addition made to the testament of Christ. But if these texts meant what Luther maintains, Christ would not have said: 'I have yet many things to say to you, but you cannot bear them now.'[21] Now Christ instituted His testament before His death. If, then, He had not said all that was to be said even at the time of His Ascension, who can deny that Christ left many other things to be afterwards added?

Moreover, if Christ wished nothing to be added

to His testament, why afterwards did He send the Spirit to lead us into all truth? Besides, why did St. Paul more than once make additions of his own, saying: 'These things I speak, not the Lord.'[22] Why did He in addition to the Scriptures hand on many other observances? For example: 'Therefore, brethren, stand firm and hold the traditions which you have learned, whether by word or by our epistle.'[23] And, again, speaking to the Corinthians about the Eucharist, he says: 'The rest I will set in order when I come.'[24] But these things were certainly never written. On this matter, however, I have written fully in my earlier book against the Lutherans.[25]

The Scriptures, then, are not to be understood in the perverse way in which Luther understands them, as if nothing whatever was to be allowed beyond what they contain, nor anything added to them, for many things besides the Scriptures have been handed down from the apostles by tradition, and many things added wisely by their successors. But rather we are to understand that nothing can be accepted which is contrary to the Scriptures, nor must anything be added which in any manner conflicts with them.

You see now, dear reader, how Luther's first attack, of which he so much boasted, lies shattered and disarmed upon the ground, utterly powerless. Let us go on to meet his second attack.

Section 23

Refutation of the authorities alleged by Luther against the priesthood in the special sense in which it is asserted in Holy Scripture. (Luther's second attack.)

TO support his second attack, which he boasts to be as formidable as the first, Luther quotes first the words of St. Paul: ' I beseech you by the mercy of God that you present your bodies a living sacrifice, holy, pleasing to God, your reasonable service.'[1]

In this passage the apostle teaches that every Christian is a priest in the same way as he is a king, not that he should rule others or administer to others the sacred rites. We, however, are speaking of priests who feed, rule and administer sacred rites to others. Unless, then, Luther can prove that each Christian has the right to rule others or be sacred ministers to them, he proves nothing.

He brings forward once more the text of St. Peter which he quoted in his first attack: ' Be you also, as living stones, built up a spiritual house, a holy priesthood, to offer up spiritual sacrifices, acceptable to God by Jesus Christ.'[2] This, too, we agree to have been said to every Christian. Every Christian is then a priest, but to himself, not for others, like those of whom we are at present speaking.

His next texts are from David—threefold, like the three kinds of sacrifices : ' A sacrifice to God is an afflicted spirit.' ' Offer to God the sacrifice of praise . . . the sacrifice of praise shall glorify me.' ' Offer up the sacrifice of justice.'[3]

I see no objection to understanding these words of the sacrifices of individual Christians, though there are some who understand the ' sacrifice of justice ' to mean the sacrifice of the Eucharist, for shortly afterwards mention is made of bread and wine, the substances by which priests offer this sacrifice. But on that point I will not argue.

His fourth text is from St. Paul : ' By Him, therefore, let us offer the sacrifice of praise to God continually, that is, the fruit of lips confessing His name.'[4]

This we have already said to be common to all Christians.

His fifth is from Osee : ' Take away all iniquity, and receive the good : and we will render the calves of our lips.'[5]

This is the sacrifice of praise which belongs to all.

The sixth is also from David : ' Thou hast broken my bonds : I will sacrifice to Thee the sacrifice of praise.'[6]

Concerning this kind of sacrifice he has already quoted above a text from the same prophet. By such texts Luther thinks that he has delivered a formidable blow. But you may see, dear reader, how unsubstantial is his attack. He has inflicted no greater a wound than could be inflicted by a weapon in the hand of a tiny child. And yet he raises a shout of triumph, as though by this one attack his victory is complete.

'Here again,' he cries, 'we will challenge the Papists to produce from the Scriptures one single jot or tittle in support of the sacrifice of their priesthood. Come now you famous priests of Baal, call upon your God.'

Come, what great blasphemy is this! Whosoever calls the priests of God priests of Baal makes Baal God. As, then, in our earlier rejoinder we proved, both from the Old and the New Testaments, that the apostles and their successors were priests of God, Luther is clearly convicted of blasphemy in calling them so insultingly priests of Baal.

And Luther goes on even to scoff at God. 'Call upon your God,' he says. 'Perhaps He is on a journey or certainly He is asleep. For He is a God and will hear. Say where it is written that Masses are sacrifices? Where did Christ teach that bread and wine were to be consecrated and offered to God?'

Upon the sacrifice of the Mass I have written much in my reply to Luther's attacks upon our most illustrious king and I imagine I have made it clear that Masses are sacrifices.[7] But how Christ consecrated bread and wine and offered them to God I have shown in my second rejoinder so fully that Luther has no growl to utter in reply. And although the apostles never mention priests under that specific name, for reasons we have already dealt with, yet under other titles they constantly speak of them. St. Peter, for example, certainly speaks of them under the name of presbyters, for he says to them: 'Feed the flock of Christ to the best of your power, taking care of it.'[8] No one, judging without prejudice, could understand these words as addressed to all Christians, for they establish an obvious distinction between the pastors and the flock.

St. Paul again speaks of them as prelates, saying: 'Obey your prelates and be subject to them, for they watch as being to render an account of your souls.'[9] Here again he clearly distinguishes them from the people for whose souls they must render an account.

Presbyters of this kind does St. Paul bid Titus ordain in every city,[10] and commend to Timothy as 'worthy of double honour,'[11] provided that they rule well.

Again, St. Paul speaks of them as 'God's coadjutors,' i.e. fellow-builders and husbandmen, whilst he calls the people the building itself and the object of the husbandman's care. For thus does he speak of himself and of those like himself: 'We are God's coadjutors'; but to the people: 'You are God's husbandry: you are God's building.'[12] For the priestly office can be described as edifying or pasturing the people, for, as St. Paul elsewhere says, they have power 'for edification and not for destruction.'[13] They are the husbandmen to whom the Lord has let out His vineyard, as we read in the Gospel: 'He will let out His vineyard to other husbandmen that shall render Him the fruit in due season.'[14] The priests of the Old Law were once the husbandmen of the Lord's vineyard. Therefore the husbandmen to whom the same vineyard is now let can be none but the priests of the New Law.

These priests, at their ordination, without doubt

received grace by the imposition of hands, as of old Timothy received it at his ordination,[15] or as those who after prayer and fasting were ordained by the imposition of hands by Paul and Barnabas.[16] For to all such apply the words which St. Paul addressed to the assembled priests of Ephesus: 'Take heed to yourselves and to all the flock, over which the Holy Ghost hath placed you bishops to rule the Church of God which He hath purchased with His own blood.'[17] Note how their ordination is ascribed not to men but to the Holy Ghost and how these words obviously establish a difference between priests and people.

Forgive me, dear reader, for repeating this so many times, but I am forced to do so by the vain boasting of Luther. Would that I could, by recalling and insisting upon these things so often, confound his arrogance in impudently maintaining that there is no difference between priests and people. The distinction leaps to our eyes on every page of the New Testament. Who is so dull as not to know the difference between the vineyard and its cultivator, the field and the husbandman, the building and the builder, the flock and the shepherd, in a word, between those who are ruled and their ruler? But constantly we read that the people are spoken of under the figure of a vineyard, field, building, flock, or are called subjects, whilst those whom before we referred to as mediators between Christ and the people are called vine-dressers, husbandmen, builders, shepherds, prelates and rulers. Who cannot see the difference?

Both, then, from the New and the Old Testament we have proved the existence of a special priesthood and confuted the reasons and scriptural texts which Luther has adduced to the contrary. What we have said is abundantly sufficient to confound Luther's second attack, and we do not know what more one could ask of us.

Section 24

Refutation of the reasons alleged to prove that the office of teacher is common to all Christians. (Luther's third attack.)

WE need not long delay upon the third attack which Luther launches against the priesthood, for he does no more than attempt to prove that the office of teacher is common to every Christian. But as this was included in his first violent attack which we have already repulsed we need not waste many words upon it now. We will pass over his trifling, his abuse, and his irrelevancies and deal only with those points which do have at least the appearance of a valid argument.

Thus does Luther, according to his wont, boast. ' We shall first prove by the irrefragable words of Scripture, that the sole legitimate ministry of the word is common to all Christians, as is the priesthood and the sacrifice. For St. Paul says : " Who hath made us fit ministers of the New Testament, not of the letter, but of the Spirit."[1] This he says of all Christians that he may make all ministers of the Spirit. For he who hands on the word of grace is a minister of the Spirit, as he is a minister of the letter who hands on the word of the law. Moses was the latter, Christ the former.'

We answer that anyone who will attentively read the chapter from which Luther has taken this text will see that St. Paul speaks here not of all Christians, but in his own person. It is obvious from the beginning of the chapter: 'Do we begin again to commend ourselves? Or do we need (as some do) epistles of commendation to you, or from you? You are our epistle, written in our hearts, which is known and read by all men: you declaring that you are the epistle of Christ, ministered by us, and written not with ink but with the spirit of the living God; not in tables of stone but in the fleshy tables of the heart.'

So far I suppose no one will deny that all is spoken by St. Paul in his own person about the ministry which he exercised in regard to the Corinthians. He goes on speaking of the same ministry, for it is without any interruption that he continues: 'And such confidence we have through Christ towards God, not that we are sufficient to think anything of ourselves, as of ourselves, but our sufficiency is from God, who hath also made us fit ministers of the New Testament, not of the letter but of the Spirit.' Here, then, as must be obvious, he is speaking of the ministration of the Gospel by which he converted the Corinthians to the faith. But notice, dear reader, how impudently Luther attempts to distort the meaning of so clear a passage. When he acts so shamelessly in regard to what is so obvious, how shall we trust him when he comes to explain passages that are obscure? St. Paul, then, in this passage, both in the earlier and the latter parts, speaks, without any change, in his own person.

Note, too, that in the following chapter he writes:
'Therefore, seeing we have this ministration, according as God hath had mercy on us, we faint not, but we renounce the hidden things of dishonesty, not walking in craftiness nor adulterating the word of God, but by manifestation of the truth commending ourselves to every man's conscience in the sight of God. And if our gospel be also hidden, it is hidden to those who perish.' Thus does he continue to speak of the ministry which was committed to him of teaching the Gentiles. So far, then, is this passage from helping Luther that it tells heavily against him. For not only in this place does he claim that to him is committed the ministry of evangelical teaching, but in almost all his Epistles he does the same. He uses similar words, for example, in his first Epistle to the Corinthians when he says: ' Let a man so look upon us as the ministers of Christ and the dispensers of the mysteries of God.'[2] And that these words are not to be understood of all Christians, but of St. Paul and Apollo alone, is clear from what follows a little further on: 'These things, brethren, I have in a figure transferred to myself and to Apollo, for your sakes.'[3] And in the previous chapter he calls them both ministers of Christ. ' Who,' he says, ' is Paul? Who is Apollo? The ministers by whom you have believed.'[4] But this ministry was not an office common to every individual member of the people, as I trust I have already shown clearly enough. False, then, is Luther's impudent assertion that St. Paul in this text was speaking of all Christians.

Luther goes on : ' Peter again says to all Christians that they should " declare His virtues who hath called you out of darkness into His admirable light."⁵ Now, every Christian has been called out of darkness. He has, then, the right, the power and the obligation to declare the virtues of Him who has called him.'

I do not imagine that St. Peter by these words meant that all Christians were to preach to the people. For he himself clearly teaches that this is the office of the pastors. Thus: ' The presbyters that are among you I beseech, who am myself also a presbyter, feed the flock of Christ to the best of your ability, taking care thereof.'⁶ To feed, that is, to teach, to rule, and to take care of the flock, is the office of the presbyters, not of every individual member of the flock. The flock has rather to be ruled, to be taught, to be cared for. No one may take upon himself the office of teacher unless he be called, however clever or learned he may be. This is the teaching of Luther himself in his commentary on the Galatians, unless he refuses to acknowledge his own words.

' Some,' he writes, ' if they do not teach, imagine foolishly that they are hiding the money of their Lord and are thus deserving of damnation. O my simple brother, one word of Christ's may deliver you from this scruple. See how the Gospel speaks : " Calling his servants, he delivered to them his goods."⁷ " Calling," he says. But who has called you ? Wait for your call, and meanwhile rest secure. Even if you are wiser than Solomon or David, yet if you are not called avoid preaching like hell. If God needs you He will call you ; if not, keep your knowledge to yourself. You will not burst.'

Therefore even Luther himself agrees that no one has any right to teach uncalled, as we have fully shown in the sixth axiom. And if it be unlawful to the clever and the learned, still more is it so to the unlearned who will ever be numerous in Christ's flock. The words, then, that we are considering do not mean that every Christian is publicly to preach the Gospel of Christ, but to bear witness to Him rather by his life and example, as indeed is said a verse or two later: 'Having your conversation good among the Gentiles, that whereas they speak against you as evil-doers, considering you by your good works they may glorify God in the day of visitation.' Surely that is to declare His virtues who called them out of darkness into His admirable light. The text of St. Peter, then, does not help Luther.

He goes on: 'We grant that all should not speak simultaneously, even though all have the same right to speak. Thus Paul was the leader of the word, and whilst he spoke Barnabas was silent.[8] But had Barnabas not also the right and the duty to speak?'

I answer that Barnabas had indeed the right and the duty to speak, because he had been separated by the Holy Ghost unto this ministry together with St. Paul, but it does not follow that individual Christians, who have not been sent nor have received the grace of teaching, have the right and power to teach.

Luther proceeds: 'Of course, as the apostle says, all things must " be done decently and according to order."[9] But this does not deny an equal ministry to all, rather it confirms it. An order in speaking must be observed, just because all have the power to speak. For if one alone had such power, what need would there be to lay down any rule as to order?'

I reply that St. Paul wished things to be done in order where there were many teachers and prophets, as would be the case in large cities, especially at Corinth, which was the metropolis of Achaia and a most famous mart for all Asia. But this does not show that each one of the townsfolk was to have an equal power of teaching.

'But,' says Luther, 'let us see the whole passage of the apostle, which like a mighty thunderbolt shatters the Papistical lies about the right and authority of teaching. "If any speak in a tongue, let it be by two or at the most by three, and in turn, and let one interpret. But if there be no interpreter, let him hold his peace in the Church and speak to himself and to God. And let the prophets speak, two or three, and let the rest judge. But if anything be revealed to another sitting, let the first hold his peace. For you may all prophesy one by one, that all may learn and all may be exhorted." '[10]

This passage seems to Luther a most mighty thunderbolt, and I partly believe it, for it has blinded him so effectually that he is unable to perceive the truth. For earlier in the same Epistle St. Paul has shown clearly enough that it is not the office of all to teach or to prophesy. 'Are all apostles?' he asks. 'Are all prophets? Are all teachers?'[11] But all would, of course, be teachers if all had the power and right to teach.

But even if we granted to Luther that they had the power to teach, they would obviously have it only in the same way as an unlearned man would have it if he were appointed to a professor's chair. He would have the right to teach, but knowing nothing, would be unable to do so. Such were most of the Corinthians, as St. Paul clearly shows: 'And I, brethren, could not speak to you as to spiritual, but as to carnal. As to little ones in Christ, I gave you milk to drink, not meat. For you were not able as yet, but neither indeed are you now able.'[12] So, then, most of the Corinthians were carnal and infants in Christ who were not yet fit for nourishment. And though they were not yet strong enough to understand what they were taught, yet these were the people whom Luther shamelessly asserts to have been fit to teach others.

'I challenge you,' says Luther, 'ye idols of the Pope. What can you mumble against this? Paul says that all can prophesy, and in order, one after the other. If to a listener anything is revealed he may rise from his seat, and the previous speaker must yield to him and be silent. All who speak are to be judged by the hearers and to be subject to their authority.'

St. Paul is speaking of the prophets and of those able to prophesy, not of the others who had not received the office of prophesying, who were, as we have shown from the words of the apostle, the great majority amongst the Corinthians. Those who were prophets and knew how to prophesy were, according to St. Paul's desire, to speak in order unless, as often happened in those days, to one were granted a special revelation. In that case St. Paul seems to have wished that the order should be interrupted and that all should listen to the new speaker whilst the earlier one kept silent.

But what has this to do with the Pope? Unless, perhaps, in a council where the Pope is present someone should receive a revelation concerning the matter in hand. In that case no one will deny that all, even the Pope, ought to listen to him and to judge whether what he brings forward is truly revealed by God.

'Where now,' says Luther, 'is your impudent mouth, your cheeks swollen out with blasphemy as with the sea, belching forth with ungovernable pride. "Where there is superiority there is authority to command, there is for all others the obligation of obedience." Satan himself speaks through your mouth these mad words against Christ speaking through Paul. Christ by His divine authority made you and yours subject to all Christians, giving to all the right to speak and to judge. But you in your effrontery make everyone subject to yourself, and, arrogating to yourself alone the right of speaking and of judging, raise yourself alone above all, like Lucifer. All Christians, then, have the right and office of teaching, to the confusion of Behemoth and all his scales.'

All this is pure abuse, unworthy of a reply. Unless there were in the Church authority to command, St. Paul would never have said: 'Obey your prelates and be subject to them.'[13] Or again: 'Let the priests who rule well be esteemed worthy of double honour.'[14] And again: 'Treat with honour such as he is.'[15] Once more: 'We beseech you, brethren, to know them who labour among you and are over you in the Lord and admonish you, that you esteem them most highly.'[16]

Never does St. Paul command otherwise, and

indeed more than once he speaks of his authority and of the obedience others must give. For there must be in the Church superiority and the authority to command. And if such authority be granted to any, most of all is it proper for it to belong to the supreme pontiff. But Luther tries to sweep away all other authority that he may reign alone. For unless I am much mistaken, he desires just what he objects to in the Pope, the subjection of all to himself. Is not this the reason why he prefers the judgement of the rude and ignorant populace to the interpretations of the holy Fathers? To him the judgement of the populace is of more weight because it approves his faction than the unanimous consent of the holy Fathers because they entirely disprove all his dogmas.

If, then, one wishes to retort Luther's abuses upon him one will find that they fit no one else so exactly. An impudent mouth, blasphemous cheeks, the belching of ungovernable pride, a tongue inflamed by Satan against Christ speaking through St. Paul, the vomiting of mad words, the effrontery of wishing to subject all things to himself, an ambition greater than Lucifer's, by which he tries to be raised up above the Pope and all the Fathers, an immeasurable arrogance by which he shamelessly despises the judgements of all men, however holy or learned. In fine, like a veritable Behemoth, he is covered by the impenetrable scales of deceit. But we have thought it right to abstain from abuse.

'Consequently,' Luther goes on, 'the words of Christ, "He that heareth you, heareth Me,"[17] are unfairly distorted to support the Pope's tyranny, just as the words of the prophet, "Touch not my anointed."[18] For when the prophet speaks of " my anointed " he means those whom God has anointed Himself and sanctified by the Holy Ghost. But the Papists restrict the words to those who are anointed with corruptible oil upon the tips of their fingers by Popes and bishops. See how wickedly the Papists treat the words of God. The anointed of God are all holy Christians, but the Pope makes adulterers and thieves the Lord's anointed.'

It is true that here the prophet speaks literally of the whole people of the Jews. The priests among them were anointed, the people were not anointed. Here, however, the prophet calls them all christs, or anointed, because of their mutual communion. We must not infer, however, that the offence of one who should strike one of the people was as heinous before God as if he had struck one of the priests. So, too, must we think of Christians of whom spiritually these words are to be understood. Amongst them there are priests and there is the people. All have been anointed and received the imposition of hands, yet because priests have twice been anointed and have been consecrated by a second imposition of hands, to them applies more strictly the command of God that His anointed are not to be touched.

Luther proceeds : ' Whereas all Christians should be heard, i.e. all who announce Christ, the Pope restricts it to his emissaries alone who announce none but the devil. Then he who despises the devil is judged to have despised his Christ.'

Surely if Luther were not inspired with an utterly diabolical spirit he would not so untruthfully interpret the Gospel. For St. Luke most clearly testifies that Christ said these words to the seventy disciples when He sent them out to preach. For thus he writes: 'After these things the Lord Jesus appointed also seventy others, and He sent them two and two before His face into every city and place whither He Himself was to come.'[19] It was to these that after many instructions He said: 'He that heareth you heareth Me, and he that despiseth you despiseth Me.' Now, if these words were said to all Christians, so must all the preceding words have been. Therefore this, too, was said to all, viz., 'Carry neither purse, nor scrip, nor shoes, and salute no man by the way'—which is obviously false.

Similar words, indeed, are related by St. Matthew to have been uttered to the apostles when they were sent out to preach: 'He that receiveth you, receiveth Me; and he that receiveth Me, receiveth Him that sent Me';[20] but as both the apostles and the seventy disciples were being sent out upon the ministry of the word, what was said of the former can well be understood of the latter.

What Luther goes on to say about man being taught by God is utterly unreasonable.[21] For since he teaches that every one of the people is taught by God, it follows that no one need obey and no one has any right to command. How foolish, then, were the Thessalonians in obeying the commands of St. Paul, as he testifies: 'We have confidence concerning you in the Lord, that the things which we command you both do and will do.'[22] Foolish too, the Philippians to whom he says: 'You have always obeyed, not as in my presence only, but much more now in my absence.'[23] Foolish also

§ 24] THIRD REJOINDER 127

the Corinthians, for he says: 'I praise you, brethren, that in all things you are mindful of me, and keep my ordinances as I delivered them to you.'²⁴ Idly did St. Paul bid Titus admonish the Christians ' to be subject to princes and powers '²⁵ and to obey the magistrates. Idly, too, did the apostles who remained in Jerusalem command the Christians who were abroad to ' abstain from blood and from things strangled '²⁶ as to which Christ left no command. Luther, of course, knows quite well that not all his Lutherans are taught by God, but he has one single aim. He wants to appear especially taught by God beyond all others and therefore subject to none; he wants to be regarded as better than all others and the master of all.

Then he puts to himself the objection that women are forbidden to teach. It seems, then, that they do not share in the ministry of the word which he contends is the common right of all Christians. With many words, then, he tries to prove that women *may* teach, that they have an equal right in this matter with men, although on account of certain difficulties they yield their right to others. And if one asks how, if women have such a right, St. Paul could take it away from them, Luther is ready with his lying glosses, viz. that St. Paul does not seem to have taken away the right from them absolutely, but only in those places where there are men able to speak, so that all things may be done decently and in order.

Good God! How shamelessly Luther distorts the Scriptures and twists them to his pleasure! Study the words of St. Paul and you will see that it is God rather than the apostle who has forbidden women this power. For shortly after he tells the Corinthians that it is the precept not of man but of God. Hear the whole passage: 'Let your women keep silence in the churches, for it is not permitted to them to speak, but to be subject as also the law saith. But if they would learn anything, let them ask their husbands at home, for it is a shame for a woman to speak in the church. Or did the word of God come out from you? Or came it only unto you? If any man seem to be a prophet or spiritual let him know the things that I write to you that they are the commands of the Lord.'[27] See, dear reader, how St. Paul first imposes silence upon women and shows that it is not so much by his own command as by the command of the law. 'They must be subject as the law saith,' i.e. the law does not permit them to speak. For God said to the woman: 'Thou shalt be under thy husband's power, and he shall have dominion over thee.'[28] And if they are doubtful about any point, may they not put a question? St. Paul replies: 'If they would learn anything, let them ask their husbands at home.' See, dear reader, that not only does St. Paul forbid them to teach, but he will not even allow them to put a question in church about necessary things. He even adds that it is a shame for women to speak in the assembly. But if perchance the Corinthians should be unwilling to listen to his admonition and wish to continue to act as they had been accustomed to do, yet as they were not the first nor the only ones to embrace the Christian faith he shows that they were bound to conform themselves to the rites of other churches, especially as it was the precept of God which he was giving them to observe. Clearly, then, the right of teaching publicly is withheld from women, since by the precept of God even the right of speaking in the church is taken from them.

And yet Luther obstinately insists that women may prophesy and teach, bringing forward some texts to support his contention. It is to be noted that the word 'prophesy' is taken in different senses. Sometimes it means in the fulness of the Spirit to praise God. Thus those upon whom after Baptism St. Paul imposed hands are said to have prophesied.[29] For in those days it was a common thing for those, upon whom the Spirit came, to speak with tongues and prophesy, i.e. to announce the wonderful works of God, as we read in various places in the Acts of the Apostles.[30] A second meaning is the foretelling of the future. Thus Agabus is said to have prophesied.[31] A third meaning is the interpretation of Scripture and of tongues, as it is more frequently used by St. Paul.

Hence it will be clear that Luther's texts will not help him. First he quotes Joel: 'And your daughters shall prophesy.' But St. Peter teaches us that this was fulfilled on the day of Pentecost when the Holy Ghost came down visibly upon the apostles and the other believers. 'This is,' he says 'that which was spoken of by the prophet Joel: And it shall come to pass in the last days (saith the Lord) I will pour out of my Spirit upon all flesh. And your sons and your daughters shall prophesy.'[32] But this kind of prophecy is merely to tell of the wonderful works of God, as we have said. It is quite different, then, from the office of a public teacher.

What Luther says of the four daughters of

Philip,[33] of Mary the sister of Moses,[34] of Holda,[35] and of Debbora[36] is nothing to the purpose, for none of these held the office of public teacher, but either prophesied of future events or gave private admonitions.

But as to the most Blessed Virgin, who bore for us the Lord Jesus, we need have no surprise if she, by a special privilege, still teaches the whole Church by her canticle. Can we wonder if she, the Mother of the Word, proclaims the word to all? Sublime beyond all others is the prerogative of the Blessed Virgin, so singular in her perfections, who alone is the Mother of God. What, then, was especially granted to her cannot be extended to others. Woe to those wretches who even in the smallest degree try to lessen the pre-eminence of this glorious Virgin, as I hear is a common practice of the Lutherans. Wherefore, unless they hasten to repent, the divine vengeance will not fail to overtake them. However, then, it may be with the most Blessed Virgin or with others, 'the privilege of the few,' as St. Jerome says, 'does not make a general law.'

What Luther last of all quotes from St. Paul is false. Nowhere does St. Paul teach that the woman must prophesy with veiled head. For if so she might teach also with veiled head, whereas St. Paul altogether forbids her to teach in the assembly. What he does say is: 'Every woman praying or prophesying with her head not covered disgraceth her head,'[37] which is quite different from what Luther says. We cannot infer that it is lawful for the woman to prophesy. St. Paul's word stands, and he is consistent with himself and with the Scriptures. He forbids altogether that women should speak to the men in church, and says that this is laid down for them by the law and by the commandment of God. Wherefore the right publicly to teach men is utterly withheld from women. Therefore the ministry of teaching is not common to all Christians.

But now let us note Luther's conclusion: 'In the strength of these indisputable texts we conclude that there is in the Church only one ministry of the word, and that common to all Christians. All may utter it, all may judge it, all must hear it. Scripture knows of no other ministry, and therefore we ask the Papistic idols whence they derive that ministry which they hold to be unshared by all. Come now, you Papists, bring forward, show me one iota of Scripture about this ministry of yours.'

See, dear reader, how Luther conjures up his female priests from nowhere. From what has been said it is abundantly clear that the ministry of pastors and rulers is not common to all Christians. But we shall not think it too much trouble to add yet one more undeniable proof that this ministry does not belong to women.

We know that many excellent women followed our Lord Jesus Christ and after His Ascension lived holily among the apostles. They had been present at our Lord's instructions, both public and private, they had witnessed His miracles, they had seen His most holy manner of life. And yet when it was a question of filling Judas' place in the ministry, St. Peter entirely excluded the women, high in sanctity though they were. 'We must choose,' he says, 'of these men who have been with us all the time that the Lord Jesus came in and went out amongst us, etc.'[38] As St. Peter so clearly teaches that a choice must be made among the men, it is obvious that women were unable to be appointed to this ministry.

You will see, dear reader, how Luther has effected nothing by his attack, for he has not shown that the ministry of the word equally belongs to all Christians, nor can he ever show it. For if, as Luther tries to prove, there were no ministry in the Church which did not belong to all equally, whether men or women, St. Peter would not have excluded women when St. Matthias was co-opted, nor would St. Paul have so often forbidden them to speak in the churches. But Luther wishes to curry favour with the ladies.

Moreover, St. Peter would have exhorted not only those who had been appointed presbyters,[39] but all Christians without distinction, to feed the flock. St. Paul, too, when he had called together at Miletus the presbyters of Ephesus would not have said especially to them: 'Take heed to yourselves and to all the flock over which the Holy Ghost hath placed you bishops to rule the Church of God which He hath purchased with His own blood.'[40] If the Holy Ghost has entrusted the Church to the rule of the presbyters it is obvious that they have a ministry which they do not share with the people. The Holy Spirit would not have distinguished between them and the flock had there not been some ministry which they held towards the flock, which the flock in return could not hold towards them.

One further point. As these priests, although ordained by the imposition of men's hands, were yet, as St. Paul here teaches, appointed by the Holy

§ 24]   THIRD REJOINDER   133

Ghost to rule the Church of God, we may be sure that whatever teaching they agreed in handing on to the churches is of the Holy Ghost. We cannot believe that so soon after the descent of the Holy Ghost any false dogma was accepted by all the churches.

St. Hegesippus testifies that until the time of Anicetus, whom he reckons as the eleventh Pope, the Church remained a virgin. These are his words : ' Up to that time the Church remained a pure and undefiled virgin. As to corrupters of the truth and adulterators of the word of God, either they did not exist or, if they did, they lay hid in the caverns of the earth or in other secret places.'[41] Clearly, then, there was no open corrupter of the truth.

St. Irenæus, who had heard St. Polycarp the disciple of St. John the apostle, speaks in similar terms of the time of Soter, the successor of Anicetus. ' To Anicetus,' he writes, ' succeeded Soter, the twelfth to hold the episcopate of the apostles. He preserved in their integrity and purity those doctrines of the faith of God which the apostles had preached and handed down.'[42]

Why do we quote these passages ? In order that we may understand that teaching which is handed down unanimously by the writers of that age must be true and incorrupt. Since, then, all orthodox writers, whose writings have survived from that time, clearly testify that the presbyters were truly priests, and had a special ministry over the flock, it follows necessarily that it is an undoubted and unassailable truth. This we shall now show.

We have already quoted many writers, both Greek and Latin, and now we shall confine ourselves to the Popes who succeeded St. Peter. Of St. Clement we have spoken. To him succeeded Anacletus in whose decrees we have the following : 'The Blessed James, surnamed "the Just," the brother of the Lord according to the flesh, was ordained the first archbishop of Jerusalem by Peter, James and John. Thus to their successors they left an example that a bishop should not be consecrated by less than three bishops, the rest assenting, and the desires of the people being ascertained. Other priests should be ordained by their own bishop, the people and the rest of the priests giving their assent and celebrating the ordination fasting. Deacons should be ordained in the same way. For the bestowal of other orders, the witness of three trustworthy men, with of course the approval of the bishop, will be sufficient.'[43] And elsewhere in the same decrees : ' Dear brethren, the order of priesthood is twofold, and it must be maintained unaltered as the Lord instituted it. Now you know that the apostles were chosen and appointed by Our Lord, and afterwards sent out into various provinces to preach. When the harvest began to grow, seeing that the labourers were few, He commanded seventy disciples to be chosen to help them. The bishops take the place of the apostles, the presbyters of the seventy disciples.'[44]

To him succeeded Evaristus in whose decrees we read the following : ' We must be united, brethren both in thoughts and in acts, that, as is written, there may be in us " one heart and one soul."[45] For we know, as also we have received from our fathers, that Christ is the head and we are His members. Therefore we have one father, the Lord in heaven. But the priests, in place of Christ, exercise His office in the Church.'[46]

After him was elected Alexander, who in his decrees after he had forbidden priests to be unjustly accused by clerics, goes on to say: 'I can conceive no worse evil than that Christians should foster ill-will towards their priests.'[47]

Sixtus, the successor of Alexander, in his decrees writes thus: 'Dearly beloved brethren, let it be known to your wisdom that in this holy apostolic see it has been ordained by us, the other bishops and all the priests of the Lord that the sacred vessels are to be touched by none save by men consecrated to God.'[48]

Telesphorus, too, the successor of Sixtus, speaking in his decrees of priests and bishops, says: 'Those who with their own lips consecrate the body of Christ are to be obeyed and feared by all, and not to be attacked or calumniated. By them the people of the Lord desire to be blessed and to be taught the way of salvation; therefore the populace must not attack them nor be received in accusation against them. The people must be taught and corrected by the priests, not vice versa, for the disciple is not above his master. For the bishops and other priests, to whose authority the people are committed, will be unable duly to correct their subjects if they know that they are attacked by insidious lies. It is just, then, that doctors of the law throughout the whole world should understand the prescriptions of the law and not besmirch the priests with their lips or by any plotting. For while they try to dishonour them they dishonour and injure themselves. He, then, who attacks priests or tries to get them condemned attacks God who has appointed them.'⁴⁹

Hyginus who succeeded Telesphorus makes no mention of priests by name in his decrees, which are commonly joined with the Apostolic Canons.

Neither is there any mention of them in the decrees of Pius, the successor of Hyginus, although Yvo, the bishop of Chartres, a man of great charity, in the fifth part of his collections, records the following words of Pius: 'As he is guilty of sacrilege who devastates the Church of God, who steals its lands and destroys its property, so is he who attacks its priests. He is guilty of sacrilege and will so be adjudged.'⁵⁰ Need I add anything more?

All these Popes reigned before Soter and Anicetus and spoke of priests as we have stated. But up to their time, as we have learned from the testimony of St. Hegesippus and St. Irenæus, the Church remained a virgin, pure and undefiled. (The Church can never, indeed, become corrupt, but this is a testimony that up to this time no heresiarch had arisen in her to attempt publicly to contaminate her.) We conclude, then, that the special priestly ministry was not at that time common to all the people.

This is a divine ordinance and with obvious reason. The people are like a flock over which the priests are placed as shepherds and rulers. Therefore did Christ thrice say to St. Peter: 'Feed My sheep.'⁵¹ And just like sheep when their shepherds are absent they suffer from many evils. For some wander away and become separated from the rest of the flock, some fall sick and, unless a remedy be at once applied, become incurable. Others are devoured by wolves or other wild beasts. Others, because they are not fed and watered at proper times, perish of hunger and thirst. So, too, of the people, unless protected by the diligent care of their pastors, some contract diseases of the soul and give way to every kind of crime, some are pitifully harried and destroyed by heretics and schismatics. Many perish of hunger and thirst because they are deprived of the word of God. Multitudes wander in the desert, and stray far from the straight path, according to the proverb of Solomon : ' Where there is no governor the people shall fall.'[52]

Men might be bold enough to deny the truth of this picture were it not that we see it daily enacted before our eyes. Where the priests feed the flock committed to them both by their word and by their example the people are preserved from many errors. But on the other hand when the priests are negligent in the performance of their duties the people fall headlong into the abyss of all evils. For this reason did Christ, even when His flock was still quite small, appoint twelve apostles and add to them seventy disciples, commanding them all to teach the people. Upon St. Peter, indeed, whom He made the chief pastor of His flock, He especially enjoined this duty, that if he loved Him he should diligently feed His flock. In addition, power was given to the apostles, either through Christ or through the Spirit of Christ, to consecrate priests as they judged fit and to place them in authority over the churches. Nor was there lacking the promise of grace as often as they should for this purpose impose hands upon anyone.

Section 25
EPILOGUE

BY this time you will, I hope, understand, dear reader, and quite clearly, that all the boasting which Luther has belched out against the sacred priesthood has come to nothing. How stands now his impudent assertion that there is no visible priesthood except what has been set up by the lies of men and by Satan? For we have abundantly proved that the priesthood is something not common to all Christians, and that it is of divine institution. Even if in the Scriptures priests were never mentioned by name, there is so much about the substance of their office that it would be more than foolish to assail it. But as now both the substance and the name are asserted in the Scriptures, as so many early writers are unanimous in their testimony to the priesthood, and there is no writer, either ancient or modern, who disagrees, as no reason or text can be adduced to the contrary, what can be more mad or shameless than to cast a shadow of doubt upon this luminous truth?

Now, then, we have established the priesthood, and from this truth necessarily flows all that is taught by the Fathers concerning the sacrifice of the Mass. There is no need here to refute all Luther's foolish blasphemies against the Mass, for we have dealt with the subject fully elsewhere, i.e. in the apology, in which we refuted Luther's attacks upon the book of our most illustrious and learned king.[1] Now let us end our treatise.

NOTES

Notes on Section 2

¹ John xx, 22.
² 1 Tim. iv, 14.
³ *Quaestiones Veteris et Novi Testamenti*, c. 93, P.L. xxxv, 2287.
⁴ Sometimes printed as *Epist. ad Evangelum Presbyterum*, P.L. xxii, 1192. St. Jerome is considered to have minimized the difference between bishops and simple priests. A discussion of his position will be found in *Dict. de Théol. Cathol.*, s.v. *Jérôme (saint)* col. 965—76, or in Moran's *Government of the Church in the First Century*, Dublin, 1913, pp. 235 et seq.
⁵ Phil. i, 1.
⁶ Acts xx, 28.
⁷ P.L. xvii, 470.
⁸ The short treatise *De Dignitate Sacerdotali* is found in all editions of St. Ambrose's works, though under many different titles. It is generally agreed that it cannot be the work of the Saint. It is printed in P.L. xvii, 567.
⁹ St. Paulinus was first banished to Phrygia, the haunt of the heretics, Montanus (this is the correct form, though the text quoted by Fisher and printed by Migne has ' Montanae ') and Maximilla, and afterwards beyond the confines of the Empire.
¹⁰ P.L. ix, 588.
¹¹ The 68th Psalm according to the Hebrew is in our version the 67th. The verse referred to (v. 31) runs thus in our Douay bible : ' Rebuke the wild beasts of the reeds, the congregation of bulls with the kine of the people.' An edition of these commentaries on the Psalms was issued at Basle in 1522 and may have been used by Fisher. P.L. liii, 49.
¹² Letter to Florentinus Pupianus. P.L. iv, 407. The first sentence seems to be given by the Saint as spoken to him by Christ in a vision. We have translated Fisher's

'omnia,' i.e. 'all things,' though the text printed by Migne has 'somnia.'

[13] Apoc. i, 6.

[14] P.L. ii, 947. We read, with the text printed by Migne, 'peraequationem' instead of 'peregrinationem.'

[15] P.G. xlv, 251. The book is entitled *De his qui in fide dormierunt*. It is very doubtful whether it is a genuine work of the Saint. A Latin translation was published in 1520 by Œcolampadius (who had not yet apostatized) and may have been the one used by Fisher.

[16] Matt. x, 8.

[17] Printed in Labbei Concil. iv, 1025.

[18] 1 Tim. iii, 3. Cyril is in error for Origen. P.G. xii, 475.

[19] Luke xvi, 10, 11.

[20] Acts xiii, 2.

[21] 1 Tim. iv, 14. The quotation continues, 'which was given thee by prophecy.' St. John Chrysostom's words will be found in P.G. lxii, 525.

[22] P.G. xxxvii, 1227.

[23] The question is amongst the *Regulae brevius tractatae*. P.G. xxxi, 1283.

[24] Cf. 1 Cor. iv, 1.

[25] Matt. iii, 6.

[26] Acts xix, 18.

[27] *Hist. Eccl.*, iii, c. 23.

[28] Ibid., x, c. 3. This is the foundation of the facts alleged, but Fisher draws from an elaboration of the original by Rufinus of Aquileia, here and in his other extracts.

[29] Ezech. xxxvii, 7.

[30] Ps. cxlviii, 12.

[31] 1 Cor. xiv, 29.

[32] Num. xi, 29.

[33] Cf. 1 Cor. xiv, 26.

[34] Rom. xii, 10.

[35] P.G. xii, 469.

[36] 1 Tim. iii, 7.

[37] The quotation is from Eusebius, *Hist. Eccl.*, iv, c. 22.

[38] The quotation is from what Lightfoot calls the 'Long Recension,' a medieval paraphrase of St. Ignatius. It is printed in *Patres Apostolici*, edit. J. B. Cotelerius—J. Clericus, Amsterdam, 1724. I, 148.

[39] Cf. Is. lxii, 11.
[40] Prov. xxiv, 21.
[41] Col. i, 15.
[42] *Patres Apostolici*, edit. cit. II, 188.
[43] Ep. viii. In edit. 1541 (Compluti), folio 140.
[44] Luke xi, 18.
[45] From Eusebius, *Hist. Eccl.*, II, c. 17. Philo is here writing of the Therapeutae. Eusebius identifies them with the Christians, but some of his commentators do not.
[46] P.G. i, 481. Migne prints the Epistle to James among the Opera Dubia of St. Clement.
[47] Matt. xxiii, 3.
[48] P.L. ii, 41.
[49] Heb. xi, 6.
[50] Ecclus. iii, 27.
[51] 1 Tim. iii, 15.

Notes on Section 3

[1] 1 Pet. iii, 18.
[2] Heb. x, 14.

Notes on Section 4

[1] 1 Tim. i, 19.
[2] 1 Tim. i, 5, 6.
[3] 2 Tim. iv, 2.
[4] 1 Cor. iii, 1, 2.
[5] Heb. v, 12.
[6] Gal. iii, 1. Cf. P.L. iv, 26.
[7] 2 Cor. xii, 20, 21.
[8] 1 Cor. x, 6–12.
[9] Heb. xii, 12.
[10] 2 Thess. iii, 11.
[11] 1 Tim. v, 13.
[12] Apoc. ii, 4.
[13] Apoc. iii, 16.
[14] Matt. xxiv, 12.
[15] Eph. vi, 11, 12.
[16] 1 Pet. v, 8.
[17] Apoc. xii, 9.

[18] Mark iv, 15.
[19] Luke xxii, 31.
[20] Matt. vii, 15.
[21] Matt. xxiv, 24.
[22] Gal. iii, 1.
[23] 1 Tim. i, 20.
[24] Acts xx, 28–30.

Notes on Section 5

[1] Luke vi, 13.
[2] Mark iii, 13, 14.
[3] Matt. x, 5–7.
[4] John vi, 71.
[5] John xv, 16.
[6] John xxi, 15.
[7] Titus i, 5.
[8] Luke x, 14–19.

Notes on Section 6

[1] Ps. xviii, 2.
[2] Ibid., 5.
[3] Num. xi, 16, 17.
[4] Exod. xxxi, 1, 6.

Notes on Section 7

[1] Matt. x, 1.
[2] Ibid., 19, 20.
[3] Luke ix, 1, 2.
[4] Mark vi, 12, 13.
[5] Mark iii, 14.
[6] Luke xxii, 14–19.
[7] Matt. xvi, 19. These words were addressed to St. Peter alone, but the words of the next text from St. John, to all the apostles, St. Thomas alone being absent.
[8] John xx, 22, 23.
[9] Acts i, 1, 2. Fisher uses here the text of Erasmus, 'impertitus in hoc ipsum Spiritum Sanctum.'
[10] Mark xvi, 14, 15.
[11] Matt. xxviii, 19.

Notes on Section 8

[1] The full title of this book is *Convulsio Calumniarum Ulrichi Veleni Minhoniensis, quibus Petrum nunquam Romae fuisse cavillatus est*. It was published in 1522.
[2] Matt. xxiv, 34. Fisher applies the text widely.
[3] Matt. xxviii, 20.
[4] Eph. iv, 11–14.
[5] Rom. xii, 4–8.
[6] 1 Cor. xii, 29–31.
[7] Rom. x, 15.

Notes on Section 9

[1] Heb. v, 4–6.
[2] Matt. viii, 19, 20.
[3] Luke xix, 13.
[4] Cf. the first verse of each of his first five Epistles as arranged in our Bible and especially the Epistle to the Galatians.
[5] Acts i, 26.
[6] Acts xiii, 1–3.
[7] Acts xiv, 22.
[8] The first word of Acts xiii, 2, which our version gives as 'And as they were ministering', is in the original λειτουργούντων or 'performing the liturgy,' cf. *infra*, p. 105.
[9] Acts xiv, 25.
[10] Mark iii, 13, 14.
[11] John x, 1–3.
[12] John x, 8. The words 'before me' (πρὸ ἐμοῦ) used by Fisher are not in the Vulgate, though they have good authority in the Greek text.

Notes on Section 10

[1] There is an exception to this general statement in Acts xiii, 7, the formal change over of name occurring only in verse 9. Some have conjectured that St. Paul adopted the name of his first important convert, Sergius Paulus.
[2] Acts xiii, 1.
[3] 1 Cor. xii, 28.
[4] Acts xiv, 22.

⁵ Ibid., 25.
⁶ Rom. i, 1.
⁷ Acts xx, 28.

Notes on Section 11

¹ 1 Tim. iv, 14.
² 2 Tim. i, 6.
³ Eph. iv, 7 *et seq.*
⁴ 1 Cor. iii, 10.
⁵ Exod. xxxi, 1–3.
⁶ 1 Cor. iii, 9.
⁷ Matt. xxi, 41.
⁸ Luke iv, 18, quoting Isa. lxi, 1.

Notes on Section 12

¹ Acts viii, 17 *et seq.*
² *Hist. Eccles.*, iii, 36.
³ Acts ix, 17–18.
⁴ Acts xiii, 3.
⁵ 1 Tim. iv, 13.
⁶ Acts xvi, 3.
⁷ 1 Cor. i, 17.
⁸ Acts xvi, 1.
⁹ 1 Tim. v, 22.
¹⁰ Titus i, 5.
¹¹ Acts xiv, 22.
¹² P.L. xxiv, 591.
¹³ Acts vi, 6.
¹⁴ Ibid., 8.
¹⁵ Acts viii, 6.

Notes on Section 13

¹ Isa. lxi, 6.
² P.L. xxiv, 624.
³ P.G. i, 478. *See* Section 2, note 46.
⁴ Acts x, 13.
⁵ Ps. cix, 4.
⁶ Heb. v, 6.
⁷ Gen. xiv, 18.
⁸ P.L. xxii, 678. Often quoted as *Epist. ad Evangelum.*

[9] This phrase is a gloss which slipped into the text of the edition of 1496 of St. Jerome—no doubt the edition used by Fisher.
[10] P.L. xxxiv, 111.
[11] *Epist. ad Caecilium.* P.L. iv, 377.
[12] Prov. ix, 1–5.
[13] St. Cyprian here quotes the LXX text which differs from the Vulgate but suits better Fisher's purpose.
[14] P.L. xvi, 438. It is very doubtful whether this treatise, *De Sacramentis*, is the genuine work of St. Ambrose.
[15] P.L. liii, 496.
[16] P.G. liii, 328.
[17] P. G. xciv, 1150.
[18] Judges ix, 13.
[19] Ps. lxxi, 16. The meaning of the Hebrew is very doubtful. Fisher's version is not from the Vulgate. It is somewhat like the A.V.
[20] Luke xxii, 19.

Notes on Section 14

[1] Heb. v, 1.

Notes on Section 15

[1] 1 Pet. iii, 18.
[2] Heb. x, 14.
[3] The book is quoted briefly as *Contra Captivitatem Babylonicam*, and was issued simultaneously with this work. (*See* Preface, p. vii.) Chapter VI proves the Mass to be a sacrifice.
[4] Isa. lxv, 24.
[5] Isa. liv, 13.
[6] Jer. xxxi, 34.
[7] Isa. xi, 9.
[8] John vi, 45.
[9] John xxi, 17.
[10] 1 Pet. v, 2 and 4.
[11] 2 Tim. iv, 1, 2.
[12] Titus i, 9.
[13] 2 Cor. v, 6.

Notes on Section 16

[1] Rom. v, 2.
[2] Rom. xv, 30.

³ 2 Cor. i, 11.
⁴ Col. iv, 3.
⁵ Eph. vi, 18, 19.

Notes on Section 17

¹ Isa. lxv, 24.
² Ibid., 18–20.
³ Rom. i, 10.
⁴ 2 Thess. i, 11.
⁵ 1 Tim. ii, 1.
⁶ 2 Tim. i, 3.

Notes on Section 18

¹ Isa. liv, 13.
² Isa. lxv, 19, 20.
³ Isa. liv, 9.
⁴ Ibid., 11, 12.
⁵ Apoc. xxi, 19, 20.
⁶ Ibid., 4.
⁷ Isa. liv, 13, 14.

Notes on Section 19

¹ Jer. xxxi, 34.
² Heb. viii, 11.
³ Fisher refers to the Sermon on the Mount. Matt. v, vi.
⁴ P.L. xliv, 225.
⁵ 1 Cor. xiii, 8.
⁶ John xvii, 3.
⁷ 1 John iii, 2.
⁸ 1 Cor. xiii, 12.
⁹ Heb. v, 12.
¹⁰ Gal. vi, 1.

Notes on Section 20

¹ Isa. xi, 9.
² Rom. x, 18.

Notes on Section 21

¹ John vi, 45.
² Eph. ii, 8.
³ Acts xx, 35.

NOTES ON SECTION 22

1 Gal. iii, 28.
2 Eph. iv, 11.
3 1 Cor. xii, 29.
4 1 Pet. ii, 1–5.
5 Apoc. v, 10.
6 Apoc. xx, 6.
7 Exod. xix, 5, 6.
8 Propositions from Luther's *Babylonian Captivity* were condemned by the Sorbonne on April 15, 1521. They may be seen in Luther's works, Jena, 1566, Tom. ii, ff. 419–427. He was enraged and replied in a satirical work. (Ibid., ff. 433 *et seq.*)
9 John xvi, 13.
10 2 Tim. iv, 5.
11 Col. iv, 17.
12 Acts i, 25.
13 Acts xiii, 2.
14 1 Tim. v, 1, 2.
15 Titus i, 5.
16 1 Tim. iv, 12.
17 Acts xx, 28.
18 John xiii, 16.
19 Luke x, 1.
20 Luke xii, 32.
21 John xvi, 12.
22 1 Cor. vii, 12.
23 2 Thess. ii, 14.
24 1 Cor. xi, 34.
25 *Assertionis Lutheranae Confutatio, Nona Veritas.* Page 293 in the 1597 edition of his works.

NOTES ON SECTION 23

1 Rom. xii, 1.
2 1 Pet. ii, 5.
3 Ps. l, 19; xlix, 14, 23 and iv, 6.
4 Heb. xiii, 15.
5 Osee xiv, 3.
6 Ps. cxv, 16, 17.
7 Cf. note 3 to Section 15.

⁸ 1 Pet. v, 1 and 2. The bishop uses the version of Erasmus, 'quantum in vobis est,' instead of the more correct 'qui in vobis est,' i.e. 'which is among you.'
⁹ Heb. xiii, 17.
¹⁰ Titus i, 5.
¹¹ 1 Tim. v, 17.
¹² 1 Cor. iii, 9.
¹³ 2 Cor. x, 8.
¹⁴ Matt. xxi, 41.
¹⁵ 1 Tim. iv, 14.
¹⁶ Acts xiii, 3.
¹⁷ Acts xx, 28.

Notes on Section 24

¹ 2 Cor. iii, 6.
² 1 Cor. iv, 1.
³ Ibid., 6.
⁴ 1 Cor. iii, 4 and 5. Erasmus's version, this time more correct.
⁵ 1 Pet. ii, 9.
⁶ *See* note 8 of previous section.
⁷ Matt. xxv, 14 and 18.
⁸ Acts xiv, 11.
⁹ 1 Cor. xiv, 40.
¹⁰ Ibid., 27–31.
¹¹ 1 Cor. xii, 29.
¹² 1 Cor. iii, 1, 2.
¹³ Heb. xiii, 17.
¹⁴ 1 Tim. v, 17.
¹⁵ Phil. ii, 29.
¹⁶ 1 Thess. v, 12, 13.
¹⁷ Luke x, 16.
¹⁸ Ps. civ, 15 and elsewhere.
¹⁹ Luke x, 1.
²⁰ Matt. x, 40.
²¹ Cf. John vi, 45.
²² 2 Thess. iii, 4.
²³ Phil. ii, 12.
²⁴ 1 Cor. xi, 2.
²⁵ Titus iii, 1.

NOTES 149

[26] Acts xv, 29.
[27] 1 Cor. xiv, 34-37.
[28] Gen. iii, 16.
[29] Acts xix, 6.
[30] Acts ii, 11 and x, 46.
[31] Acts xi, 28 and xxi, 10, 11.
[32] Acts ii, 16, 17.
[33] Acts xxi, 9.
[34] Exod. xv, 20.
[35] 4 Kings xxii, 14.
[36] Judges iv, 4.
[37] 1 Cor. xi, 5.
[38] Acts i, 21.
[39] 1 Pet. v, 1.
[40] Acts xx, 28.
[41] Cf. Eusebius, *Hist. Eccl.*, iv, c. 22.
[42] Cf. P.G. vii, 851.
[43] P.G.-L. ii, 802. Migne quotes Mansi, *Eruditis Catholicis videntur suppositae*. This judgement is applicable also to the decrees that follow.
[44] Ibid., 812.
[45] Acts iv, 32.
[46] Labbeus-Mansi, Concil. Collect., I, 627.
[47] Labbeus-Mansi, ibid., 638.
[48] Ibid., 653. The fact is in the *Liber Pontificalis*.
[49] Ibid., 658.
[50] Ibid., 675. Though this letter may not be genuine, it shows the accuracy of Blessed Ivo or Yvo of Chartres (Bishop 1090 or 1092 to 1115), one of the greatest of medieval canonists. His *Liber Decretorum* was printed in 1499 at Basle, and this book was probably used by Fisher.
[51] John xxi, 17.
[52] Prov. xi, 14.

NOTE ON SECTION 25

[1] *See* Section 15, note 3.

INDEX OF AUTHORS QUOTED
(Other than Biblical).

Alexander I, Pope St., 135
Ambrose, St., 7, 69
Anacletus, Pope St., 134
Arnobius, 8, 69
Augustine, St., 5, 68, 91

Basil, St., 11

Chrysostom, St. John, 10, 69
Clement I, Pope St., 17, 64, 134
Cyprian, St., 4, 8, 68
Cyril, St., 9 (by error for Origen)

Dionysius (pseudo-), 16

Erasmus, 105
Eusebius, 12, 59
Evaristus, Pope St., 134

Fisher, John Cardinal, of Rochester, 41, 78, 109, 112, 138

Gennadius, 9
Gregory, St., Nazianzen, 11

Hadarsan, Rabbi Moses, 70
Hegesippus, St., 14, 133, 136
Hilary, St., 7

Ignatius, St., 14, 59
Irenæus, St., 133, 136
Ivo, Blessed, of Chartres, 136

Jerome, St., 6, 64, 68, 130
Johai, Rabbi, 71
John, St., Damascene, 9, 70

Kimhi, Rabbi, 72

Luther, 48, 119 and *passim*

Origen, 13, cf. Cyril, St.

Philo, 16
Pinhas, Rabbi, 71
Pius I, Pope St., 136
Polycarp, St., 15

Selemon, Rabbi, 72
Semuel, Rabbi, 70
Sixtus I, Pope St., 135

Telesphorus, Pope St., 135
Tertullian, 4, 8, 9, 20

Vulgarius, 70

The Mayflower Press Plymouth. William Brendon & Son, Ltd.

Appendix

Sermon against Luther

The text of this Sermon has been transcribed into modern English by Dr. Anne Barbeau Gardiner, Professor Emeritus of English Literature at John Jay College, New York City. Her transcription into modern English of Saint John Fisher's *Meditations on the Seven Penitential Psalms* is to be published soon by Ignatius Press. Quotations in Latin from the Scriptures are reproduced in the orthography as used by Fisher according to the custom of his times. I have supplied references to the Migne edition of the Latin and Greek Fathers. The Sermon's line of argument is so clearly stated at the very start of the First Instruction as to make unnecessary any explanatory comment. Noteworthy are Fisher's apposite quotations of the Church Fathers about the primacy of Peter and his successors, about the binding force of Tradition as handed down separately from the Scriptures, and about the misinterpretation from the earliest times of St. Paul's dictum on salvation by faith (S. L. J.).

Sermon against Luther

The Sermon of John [Fisher], bishop of Rochester, made against the pernicious doctrine of Martin Luther within the octaves of the Ascension (1521), by the assignment of the most reverend father in God the lord Thomas [Wolsey], Cardinal of York and legate *ex latere* from our holy father the pope.

Cum venerit Paraclitus, quem ego mittam vobis, Spiritum veritatis, qui a Patre procedit, ille testimonium perhibebit de me (Jn 15:26).

These are the words of our Savior Christ Jesus in the gospel of John, read in the gospel for this Sunday. In English he says: when the Comforter shall come, whom I shall send you, the Spirit of truth that proceeds from my Father, he shall give witness of me.

Very often when the day is clear and the sun shines bright, there rises in some quarter of the sky a thick black cloud that darkens all the face of heaven and shadows from us the clear light of the sun. It stirs a hideous tempest, makes a great lightning and thunders terribly, so that weak souls and feeble hearts are put in a great fear and made almost desperate for lack of comfort.

In like manner in the Church of Christ, when the light of faith (that shines from the spiritual sun almighty God) has been clear and bright for a good season, there has risen often some black cloud of heresy that stirs such a tempest, makes such a lightning, and so terribly thunders that many a weak soul has thereby gone astray.

Such a cloud was Arius, who stirred so great a tempest that it vexed the Church of Christ many years afterwards. And after him came many other similar clouds, like Macedonius, Nestorius, Eutyches, Elvidius, Donatus, Jovinianus, Pelagius, John Wycliffe, and others who every one of them sorely tempted the Church in his time. Such heretics Saint Jude in his epistle calls *nubes sine aqua, que a vento circumferuntur* (Jd 12). That is to say, they are clouds without the moisture of grace, moved by the winds of wicked spirits. And now such another cloud is raised aloft, one Martin Luther a friar, who has stirred a mighty storm and tempest in the Church, has shadowed the clear light of many divine scriptures, and makes a perilous lightning issue from him, that is to say, a false light of wrong understanding of scriptures, a light which does not issue from the Spirit of truth but from the spirit of error and from the spirit of this tempest, his most perilous heresy. Furthermore, he thunders terribly against the pope's authority, against the general councils, against the traditions and ordinances left to us by the apostles, against the doctrine of the fathers and doctors of the Church.

Our Savior Christ, by his divine providence foreseeing that many such pestilent clouds and tempests would arise to the great trouble and vexation of his Church, out of the tender love and infinite charity which he bears towards our mother holy Church, promised that after he had ascended to his Father he would send her the Holy Spirit of God, the Spirit of truth to abide with her forever, to confirm her from time to time in the knowledge of every truth to which both she and every child of hers, that is to say every true Christian man, should give assured faith, and finally to be in all such storms her true Comforter, according to the beginning of this gospel cited above: *cum autem venerit Paraclitus, quem ego mittam vobis, Spiritum veritatis, qui a Patre procedit, ille testimonium perhibebit de me.* That is, when the Comforter comes, whom I shall send you, the Spirit of truth who proceeds from my Father, he shall give witness of me. This holy gospel graciously offers us four good instructions against these dangerous tempests of heresies whenever they happen to arise, but especially against this most pernicious tempest that Martin Luther has now stirred up.

The first three instructions, by the will of God and the help of the Holy Spirit, shall undermine the three great grounds upon which Martin Luther bases all his articles, and the fourth shall answer to the defence which his followers make for him, thereby putting many a weak soul in peril.

But before we declare these instructions, we shall make our prayer to the Holy Spirit of truth, that in this dangerous storm and perilous tempest, he will calm our hearts with the testimony of his truth, so that we shall not waver in the Catholic doctrine of our mother holy Church, but steadfastly believe such teachings as have been derived to us from our Savior Christ Jesus by his apostles and their successors, the holy bishops and fathers and doctors of the Church. For this and for the grace necessary for you and for me, let everyone make a prayer.

The First Instruction against Martin Luther

The first instruction is offered us in these first words of the gospel: *cum autem venerit Paraclitus quem ego mittam vobis, Spiritum veritatis, qui a Patre procedit*. In these words the Spirit of truth is promised us, to be our comfort in all doubtful opinions that may arise in Christ's Church. Touching this first instruction I want to do three things: first, to show that the instructions of this holy gospel pertain to the universal Church of Christ; secondly, that the head of the universal Church is the pope; thirdly, that Martin Luther (who divides himself from this head) does not have in him the Spirit of truth. For the first, Martin Luther cannot deny that this promise is made to the universal Church, for we shall bind him to it by his own reasoning in the book "Of the Captivity of Babylon" (1520): "if we will affirm that any one epistle of Saint Paul or any one place in his epistles does not pertain to the universal Church of Christ, we take away all Saint Paul's authority." Now if it is true of the words of Saint Paul, much more is it true of the gospels of Christ and of every place written in the same gospels. In the universal Church, then, this Holy Spirit of truth rests and shall continue to the world's end: *ut maneat vobiscum in eternum,* he shall abide in the universal Church forever; *et docebit vos omnem veritatem,* he shall in every doubt teach us the truth. Thus much for the first.

Now for the second, where I said that the pope *jure divino* (by divine right) is head of the universal Church of Christ. When you see a tree standing upright on the ground in the clear sunlight, with its branches spread abroad full of leaves and fruit, this tree makes a shadow. Within this shadow you may perceive a figure of the branches, the leaves, and the fruit. Everything in the tree has something corresponding to it in the shadow. And every part of the shadow has something corresponding to it in the tree. A man's eye may lead him from every part of the tree to every part of the shadow, and again from every part of the shadow to every corresponding part of the tree. Everyone may point to a particular part of the shadow and say, this is the shadow of such a branch, this is the shadow of such a leaf, this is the shadow of the trunk of the tree, and this is the shadow of the top of the tree. And so it is that the law of Moses and the government of the synagogue of the Jews was but a shadow of the government of the universal Church of Christ. So says Saint Paul, *umbram habens lex futurorum bonorum,* the law had but a shadow of the things to come (Heb 10:1). And, to the Corinthians, *omnia in figura contingebant illis* (1 Cor 10:11); all their government was but a figure and shadow of the Church. Now then, to my purpose. In their government were two heads appointed, one under another, Moses and Aaron, to conduct the people through the desert to the promised country. We understand that the Jewish people were a shadow of the Christian people and that their journey through the desert to the promised country was a shadow of our journey through this wretched world to the heavenly country. But Moses and Aaron, the heads of that people, who are they the shadow of? Without doubt they must be the shadow of Christ and of his vicar Saint Peter, who under Christ was also the head of the Christian people.

You will see this more plainly by three correspondences. First, Moses and Aaron were both of them priests. Moses was made so by God, and Aaron was made so by Moses at the commandment of God, and to Aaron was committed the cure of the Jews in the absence of Moses. Likewise, Christ and Saint Peter were both priests of the new law. Christ was made a priest by his Father almighty God, as it is written of him, *tu es sacerdos in eternum secundum ordinem Melchisedech,* you are a priest forever according to the order of Mechisedech (Ps 109:4). And Peter was made so by Christ, and to Peter Christ committed the cure of the Christian people in his absence, saying feed my sheep, *pasce oves meas pasce, pasce, pasce* (Jn 21:17). The second correspondence is this: Moses was mediator between almighty God and Aaron for the people's cause, and Aaron was mediator between Moses and the people for God's cause. So Scripture teaches that almighty God said to Moses, speaking of Aaron, *ipse loquetur pro te ad populum, et erit os tuum: tu autem eris ei in his que ad Deum pertinent.* That is to say, he shall speak in your place to the people, and you shall speak for him again in those things that pertain to God (Ex 4:16). Will you see how Christ was the mouth of Peter towards almighty God? He said to Saint Peter, *Simon, Simon, ecce Satanas expetivit vos, ut cribraret sicut triticum; ego autem rogavi pro te, ut non deficiat fides tua. Et tu, aliquando conversus, confirma fratres tuos.* That is to say, Simon, Simon, behold Satan has desired greatly to sift you as a man sifts his wheat, but I have prayed for you that your faith shall not fail; and you, once converted to the stable way, confirm your brothers (Lk 22:31-2). See now whether Christ was not here the mouth of Peter when he promoted his cause before almighty God the Father and prayed for him that his faith might not finally perish. And contrariwise, was not Peter the mouth of Christ when he, after converting to the true way, confirmed his brothers? The third correspondence is this: Moses ascended the mountain to speak with almighty God, and Aaron remained behind to instruct the people; and did not Christ likewise ascend to his Father up the mount of heaven? And for what purpose, I ask you? Saint Paul tells it, *ut appareat vultui Dei pro nobis*, to appear before the face of almighty God for us (Heb 9:24), and there to be our advocate, as Saint John says (1 Jn 2:1). And did not Peter remain behind to teach the people whom our Savior had committed to his charge, just as Aaron was left to teach the Jewish people when Moses was above on the mountain of God?

Thus, everyone may see how that shadow and this thing agree and correspond to one another fully and clearly. But now let us pause here a while. I will explain this figure by yet another deed of Christ in the gospel. The Jews had to pay taxes to the Romans, and in particular the head of every household had to pay a certain coin called didrachma. When those who were gatherers of this tax came to Saint Peter, our Savior told him that he should go to the sea, there in a fish's belly he would find staterem, which was a double didrachma, and he should give it to the tax-gatherers, both for himself and for Christ (Mt 17:26). Note here that this tribute was head money paid for those who were heads and governors of households, and that Christ commanded this to be paid for no one else except himself and Saint Peter, and thereby paid for all the other apostles. Join this fact of the gospel to the preceding figure and what can be more plain to see than that Peter, under Christ, was the head of all the household of Christ? But yet thirdly, let us hear the testimony of some father of the Church that this is the very meaning of the gospel. Saint Augustine, in question 75 of the Book of Questions of the New and the Old Testament, speaks in this manner: *didrachma capitum solutio intelligitur,* the payment of this money was head money paid for the heads of household. And this follows: *salvator quum pro se et Petro dari iubet, pro omnibus exoluisse videtur, quia sicut in salvatore erant omnes causa magisterii; ita et post salvatorem in Petro omnes continentur, ipsum enim constituit caput eorum.*[1] That is to say, when our Savior commanded this double tax to be paid for himself and for Peter, in so commanding he paid for all the remaining apostles, for they were all contained in him as their master; and as they were all contained in our Savior, so after our Savior they were all contained in Peter, for Christ made him the head of them all. Here note in Saint Augustine that because Saint Peter was head of them all and they were contained in him, this tax paid for him was therefore paid for them all. And by yet another scripture which I cited before, Saint Augustine proves that all the other apostles were contained in Saint Peter: Simon, Simon, Satan has desired to sift you as a man sifts wheat, but I have prayed for you that your faith shall not fail, and you, once you are converted to the stable way, confirm your brothers. On these words Saint Augustine said, Christ did not pray for James and John and for the others, but for Saint Peter in whom the others were contained.

Consider now how these testimonies confirm and strengthen one another: first, the figure and shadow of the old law; secondly, the testimony of the gospels answering to the same; thirdly, the declaration of Saint Augustine on the same. And here I bring but one doctor whose testimony in the balance of any true Christian man's heart, I think, should weigh down Martin Luther. But Saint Ambrose also speaks of the didrachma, calling it *capitum solutionem*, head money. And of Saint Peter he says, *Petra enim dicitur, eo quod primus in nationibus fidei fundamentum posuerit, et tanquam saxum immobile totius operis christiani compagem, molemque contineat.*[2] That is to say, Peter is called petra, because he first established the ground of our faith among the Gentiles and, as a stone not easy to be removed, contains in him and makes solid all the frame and greatness of the work of Christ. And Saint Gregory says, *certe Petrus apostolus primum membrum sancte et universalis ecclesie est. Paulus, Andreas, Joannes, quid aliud quam singularum plebium sunt capita.*[3] That is to say, Peter is the chief member of the universal Church; Paul and Andrew and John, what else are they but heads of particular and single peoples? Whereby it appears that each one was chief of the people whom he had the cure of, but Saint Peter was chief of the universal Church. Saint Jerome also says, speaking of Peter, *propterea inter duodecim unus eligitur, ut capite constituto,* *schismatis tolleretur occasio.*⁴ That is to say, Peter was chosen, one out of the twelve, to be their head and to take away all occasions of schismatic division. Furthermore, Saint Cyprian says, speaking of Peter when he confessed Christ Jesus to be the Son of God: *loquitur illic Petrus super quem edificanda fuerat ecclesia,*⁵ there speaks Peter upon whom the church was to be built. But how could the Church be built upon him if he were not the head and chief member of the Church?

All these are holy fathers of the Latin church, all men of great learning, all men of singular holiness, whose virtuous manner of living was confirmed by miracles done both while they were alive and after their death. In the Greek Church likewise, Saint John Chrysostom, after he has praised Saint Paul, speaks of Saint Peter, saying, *quod ipse qui fuit apostolorum caput talis fuit,* Saint Peter who was the head of the apostles was just such another. And he often calls Saint Peter *eximium apostolorum, et os discipulorum ac verticem collegii*⁶, that is, the chief of the apostles, the mouth of the disciples, and the top and head of all the college. And Origen says, *magno illi ecclesie fundamento petreque solidissime super quam christus fundavit ecclesiam suam, vide quid dicatur a domino: modice fidei, quare dubitasti?*⁷ That is to say, see what Our Lord said to that great foundation of the Church and most stable stone: O man of little faith, why did you doubt? If all these many testimonies both of Greeks and Latins shall not outweigh one friar, is it reasonable? I trust there is no true Christian man who will not be moved with the testimony of all these, especially when they are grounded on such a plain and evident figure of the old law and on such a clear light of the holy gospels.

But here Martin Luther will say that he cannot conceive *duos summos,* of two heads. Of this I marvel greatly. For it is manifest that Aaron was called *summus* in scripture, and if he was *summus sacerdos,* Moses was not a bit beneath him, and so then the two of them were both *summus,* one under the other, in comparison with the rest of the people. So Saint Paul speaks of many heads, saying, *caput mulieris vir, caput viri Christus, Christi vero deus* (1 Cor 11:3).

See here how a woman has three heads, God, Christ, and her husband, and yet besides all these she has a head of her own. It would be a monstrous sight to see a woman without a head. What comfort would her husband find in her? If then one woman, notwithstanding she has a head of her own to govern herself according to the will and pleasure of her husband, yet has her husband to be her head, and Christ to be her head, and God to be her head, how much more does our mother holy Church, who is the spouse of Christ, have a head of her own, that is to say the pope, and yet nevertheless Christ Jesus, her husband, is her head, and almighty God is also her head.

But now let us return to our instruction. Thus, then, you understand that the Spirit of truth remains forever in the universal Church of Christ, and that the head of this Church, under Christ, is the pope. By this briefly it may appear that the Spirit of Christ is not in Martin Luther. The spirit of every natural body gives life no farther than to the members and parts of that body which are naturally joined to the head. And so it must be likewise in the mystical body of our mother holy Church. To the extent, then, that this wretched man has divided himself from the head of this body, that is, the vicar of Christ, how can he have in him the Spirit of this body, which is the Spirit of truth? And especially when he has divided himself with such pride, arrogance, and presumption, which is most odious to this Holy Spirit, and when he so spitefully, so presumptuously, so maliciously scorns, treats as nothing, and tears into pieces the head of Christ's Church, to whom as to his chief spiritual father he has, by reason of his religion, vowed and promised obedience. How can this man have in him the Spirit of God, this Holy Spirit of truth? And here I make an end of the first instruction.

The Second Instruction against Martin Luther

For the second instruction, the next words ensue: *ille testimonium perhibebit de me,* and he shall bear witness or give evidence of me. What marvellous virtue, what wonderful activity is in the sunbeams which we see spread upon the earth at this time of year, quickening and filling with life many creatures which before appeared dead. Suppose someone who had no prior experience of this matter saw the trees in winter season when they were withered, their leaves shaken from them, all the moisture shrunk into the root, and no vigor of greenness or of life appearing outwardly, would he think it likely that the same trees could revive again and be so delightfully clad with leaves and flowers as we now see them? And yet this is done by the subtle power and secret activity of the sunbeams spread upon the earth.

Nevertheless, not every sunbeam has this virtue. Sunbeams truly shed light in winter as they do now at this time of year, but that light is so faint and feeble that it gives no life. Otherwise we would have grass and trees growing as well in winter as now at this time of year. The cause of this weakness is that the sun sails so low near the earth in winter that its beams therefore slant towards the ground and do not rebound or double themselves again towards the sun. You see, when a bowl is thrown slanting on a wall, it slides forward and does not rebound backward directly against the thrower, but when it is cast directly against a wall with great violence, then it directly rebounds again. This is the way with sunbeams: the nearer the sun draws to us now at this time of year, the more directly its beams beat on the ground and the more directly they rebound and return again towards the sun. And because of the nearness of beam to beam, a greater strength arises in the beam and a fuller light, *quia omnis virtus unita fortior est*, for every virtue that is gathered together is stronger. A single thread is nowhere as strong as a double, and a single sunbeam is nowhere as mighty as when it is doubled and turned on itself by rebounding and reflection. Furthermore, from this doubling there rises a heat and warmth which is the principal worker of life in every creature. But for all this, we are not sure any tree is alive until we see it putting forth buds and leaves.

This example, if you understand it, may induce us to conceive how wonderfully the spiritual sun almighty God works by his spiritual and invisible beams of light spread upon the soul of man or upon the Church, both of which are called in scripture a spiritual earth: *Dominus dabit benignitatem, et terra nostra dabit fructum suum*, our Lord shall give his gracious influence and our earth shall yield fruitful works (Ps 84:13). The beams of almighty God spread upon our souls quicken them and cause this life in us and the fruit of good works. First, they cause the light of faith, but this is a very slender light when it lacks the rebounding of hope and the heat of charity. Faith without hope is a slender beam and of little power. But join to it hope, which rebounds up to God again, *ad ea que non videntur*, and then is it much stronger than before. For now this faith is doubled and returned on itself and gathered nearer into itself and made more valiant and mighty than before. Before it was like the faith Saint Peter had when Christ bade him come to him upon the sea. He believed his Master, but he had no very firm hope that he could walk there. He was not strong in his faith, and therefore our Savior said to him: *modice fidei, quare dubitasti?* (Mt 14:31). But of the strong faith that has confidence and hope joined with it, he says in another place, *si habueritis fidem sicut granum sinapis, dicetis monti huic: "transi hinc illuc!", et transibit.* That is to say, if you had faith like a mustard seed, you could command this mountain to remove itself and by your faith it would depart (Mt 17:20). This is a great faith which also has confidence and hope joined with it. A mustard seed is very little, but it has a great virtue compacted and gathered within it. So when the beams of faith and hope are joined together at one point, then it is of mighty power. Sunbeams gathered together by reflection of a burning glass are so mighty they will set tinder or cloth on fire. And likewise it is of the beams of faith and hope when they are jointly compacted and united together. If a man had such a faith and confidence that he might command a great mountain to remove for his pleasure, this would be a mighty faith. Nevertheless, if a man had such a faith and lacked the heat of charity, he would be as a dead tree. For Saint Paul says, *si habuero omnem fidem, ita ut montes transferam, caritatem autem non habuero, nihil sum* (1 Co 13:2). If I have all faith—he that speaks of all leaves out none—if I have all faith, he says, and so mighty a faith that by my faith I may remove great mountains at my command, yet lack the heat of charity, I am nothing but a dead stock, a tree without life. And therefore Saint James says, *fides sine operibus mortua est*; faith without the fruit of good works is dead (Js 2:20). To this purpose our instruction says, *ille testimonium perhibebit de me*, he shall bear witness of me. Of whom? Of Christ. What is Christ? *Lux vera, que illuminat omnem hominem, venientem in hunc mundum,* the true light which enlightens every creature coming into this world (Jn 1:9). Who shall bear witness or give evidence of this light? The Spirit of God. *Quia caritas Dei diffusa est in cordibus nostris per Spiritum Sanctum, qui datus est nobis*; that is to say, the heat of the charity of God is spread in our hearts by the Holy Spirit who is given to us (Rm 5:5). The heat of charity gives evidence that the light is full of life. No matter how much light of faith a man has, unless he has also this heat of charity stirring his soul and bringing forth lively works, he is but a dead stock and a tree without life. For as I said, though the natural sun should shine ever so bright upon a tree, yet if this tree has no greenness in it, no putting forth of buds and leaves, this tree is not alive. So when the beams of the spiritual sun are spread upon our souls, if we feel not the stirring heat to do fruitful works, our souls are dead.

But now to what purpose serves this instruction? To this: it subverts one great ground of Martin Luther, which is this, that faith alone without works justifies a sinner. Upon this ground he builds many other erroneous articles and especially that the sacraments of Christ's Church do not justify, but faith alone justifies. A perilous article able to subvert all the order of the Church! But touching these sacraments, the king's grace, our sovereign lord in his own person has with his pen so substantially fought against Martin Luther that I have no doubt every true Christian man who shall read his book will see those blessed sacraments cleared and delivered from the slanderous mouth and cruel teeth that Martin Luther has set upon them, wherein all

SERMON AGAINST LUTHER 165

England may take great comfort and especially all those that love learning.[8] Plato says, *tum beatas fore respublicas quando aut philosophi regnent aut reges philosophentur*, then shall commonwealths be blessed when either those that are philosophers govern, or else those that govern give themselves to philosophy.[9] And scripture exhorts princes to the same, saying, *et nunc, reges, intelligite erudimini, qui iudicatis terram*, and now you who are kings, study to have understanding, and you that take upon you the judgments of the world, strive after learning [Ps 2:10].

But now, let us return to our matter again. For this ground Martin Luther brings Saint Paul saying in several places that a man is justified by his faith alone, without works. Nevertheless, Saint Augustine says that Saint Paul's words were misconceived from the beginning of the Church, and for this reason the other apostles in their epistles aimed at showing the opposite side.[10] But some here are thinking that Martin Luther has little regard for Saint Augustine. It is true, and yet it is a foul presumption. Let him at least believe the other apostles, whom he cannot deny without manifest heresy. Saint James says, *ex factis iustificatur homo et non ex fide tantum*, a man is justified by his deeds and not by his faith alone (Js 2:24). Not only does he say this but he proves it in several ways. One way is this: *demones credunt et contremiscunt*, the devils believe and tremble. The devils have faith, but no one can say the devils are justified by their faith. How many live in horrible sin who yet have the faith of Christ Jesus and would rather die than deny their faith? But for all that, they are not justified. If faith alone justified, both they and the devils also would be justified. Secondly, the same example Saint Paul uses to the Romans to prove that faith justifies a sinner without works, Saint James uses to the contrary, I mean the example of Abraham, which appears in the same place. But then you will say, Sir, are these apostles contradicting one another? To this, Saint Augustine says, no, truly. Rather, Saint James says the contrary only of what may be misconstrued and mistaken in Saint Paul. For Saint Paul means the works that go before faith, and Saint James means the works that follow after faith. Saint Paul means that for the justifying of Abraham, it was not necessary for the work of circumcision or the other works of the law to come before faith, for his faith justified him without them (Rm 4:9-13). Saint James means that the fruitful works which follow after faith and give evidence of a lively faith justify a man. And if Abraham had not had these, he says, he would not have been justified. If Abraham had not been ready to offer up his son Isaac at the command of God, he would not have been justified. But because he was ready, he says, therefore, Abraham *ex operibus iustificatus est*, Abraham was justified by his works (Js 2:21). Thus, Saint James speaks not against Saint Paul but against the misunderstanding and misconceiving of him. Of which misconceiving Saint Peter also speaks in his second epistle, saying, *in quibus sunt quedam difficilia intellectu que indocti et instabiles depravant sicut et ceteras Scripturas ad suam ipsorum perditionem*; that is to say, in the epistles of our very dear brother Paul are some things hard to be conceived, which unstable minds misconstrue, as they do many other scriptures, to their own damnation (2 Pt 3:16). You may thus see that several others have misconstrued Saint Paul before now, as Martin Luther does to his own peril and damnation.

But here is one thing that I especially marvel at in Martin Luther: he says that in all scripture there is no other testimony against him except this one place in Saint James. But undoubtedly many more testimonies may be brought. And first, our Savior in the gospel of Luke says, *date eleemosynam et ecce omnia munda sunt vobis,* give alms and all things shall be clean to you (Lk 11:41). What is this cleanness but the justifying of our souls, which is promised for the works of almsgiving? If I believe ever so much but I relieve not the poor in their necessity, I shall not attain to this cleanness. Furthermore, in the gospel of Matthew, *si remiseritis hominibus errata sua remittet & vobis pater vester celestis, quod si non remiseritis hominibus errata sua nec pater remittet vobis errata vestra.* That is to say, if you forgive those who have grieved you by their offences, your Father in heaven shall do likewise, but if you do not forgive those who have grieved you by their offences, your

Father shall not forgive you your offences done against him (Mt 6:14). In addition, he says in the same gospel, *non omnis, qui dicit mihi: "Domine Domine", intrabit in regnum celorum, sed qui facit voluntatem Patris mei* (Mt 7:21). That is to say, if we work not the will of almighty God the Father, we shall not be justified, nor enter into the kingdom of heaven. Besides these, in the same gospel, *nisi abundaverit iustitia vestra plus quam scribarum et phariseorum, non intrabitis in regnum celorum*, unless your justice or your manner of living is better and more ample than was the justice and living of the Jews and Pharisees, you shall not enter into the kingdom of heaven (Mt 5:20). This is to be understood *de justitia operum,* of the justice of works, as clearly appears from all that follows. Besides this he says, *omnis qui audit verba mea hec et non facit ea, similis erit viro stulto, qui edificavit domum suam supra arenam,* all who hear my words and do not work accordingly are like an unwise man who builds his house upon unsure ground (Mt 7:26). And Saint Paul also says, *non auditores legis sed factores iustificabuntur*, such as are only hearers of the law of God shall not be justified, but such as are workers thereafter (Rm 2:13). And Saint James says, *estote factores verbi et non auditores tantum fallentes vosmetipsos,* be workers of the word of God and not only hearers, or you deceive yourselves (Js 1:22). And Saint Paul again says, *si secundum carnem vixeritis, moriemini; si autem Spiritu facta carnis mortificatis, vivetis*; that is to say, if you live after the works of your flesh, you shall die; but if by the Spirit you mortify in you the works of your flesh, you shall live (Rm 8:13). And finally Saint Paul says, resolving his own sentence, *fides que per dilectionem operatur,* faith which is wrought by love (Gal 5:6). Accordingly, Saint James says (of Abraham), *vides quoniam fides cooperabatur operibus illius, et ex operibus fides consummata est*; you see how faith cooperated with his works and by works his faith was made perfect (Js 2:22). By all these testimonies you may plainly see that faith alone does not suffice, but love and works are also required for the justifying of our souls. And thus much for the second instruction.

The Third Instruction against Martin Luther

Touching the third instruction, it follows in the gospel, *et vos testimonium perhibebitis, quia ab initio mecum estis*. That is to say, you shall bear witness because you have been conversant with me from the beginning (Jn 15:27). Before whom shall they bear witness but the universal Church of Christ? Their witness then must be allowed by every true Christian man. By these words and by others cited above, it appears that more testimony must be admitted as being of sufficient authority than what is written in the Bible only. If we can establish this one thing, it will cast down a great number of Martin Luther's articles. But for this we must consider that these three Persons of whom this gospel makes mention are undivided and undissevered from one another in all their works; they jointly go together, yet scripture assigns these three Persons three different times in which they have instructed mankind of the truth necessary to be believed. First, almighty God the Father instructed our elders by his prophets, as Saint Paul says, *multifariam multisque modis olim Deus loquens patribus in prophetis*; that is to say, almighty God, the first Person in the godhead, instructed our fathers in many different ways through his prophets (Heb 1:1). By our fathers, Saint Paul here means the Jews, of whom we are spiritually descended, for Abraham who was their carnal father is our spiritual father. Now almighty God the Father taught them by his prophets, who, albeit their prophecies are written in scripture, spoke many more things which were unwritten and which were of as great authority as what was written, which the master Jews call *cabbala*,[11] something derived from man to man by mouth only and not by writing. After this, the second Person, the Son of God our Savior Christ Jesus, was sent by his Father into this world to instruct man both by himself and by his apostles, who, as the gospel here says, were conversant with him from the beginning (Jn 15:27). These blessed apostles left us also many things by mouth which are not written in the Bible. This appears in the second epistle to the Thessalonians, where Saint Paul, who came after them and was not present when Christ said those words to them, says, *state et tenete traditiones quas didicistis sive per sermonem sive per epistulam nostram.* That is to say, be constant and keep those instructions and teachings that you have learned of us either by mouth or else by writing (2 Thess 2:15). If Saint Paul (who came later than the other apostles to whom Christ said those words) will have his traditions observed and kept, both those he told them by mouth and those he wrote with his pen, why should the traditions of all the other apostles not be kept likewise and be of equal strength to make faith and to bear witness of the truth? Here you may see by the express scripture of Saint Paul that we are bound to believe many more things than are written and put in the Bible. We shall confirm this by Origen, who is an ancient doctor and to whom on this point great faith is to be given. In his fifth Homily on the Book of Numbers, he says, *sed in ecclesiasticis observationibus sunt non nulla que omnibus facere necesse est, nec tamen ratio eorum omnibus patet. Nam quod verbi gratia genua flectimus orantes, et quod ex omnibus celi plagis ad solam orientis partem conversi fundimus orationem, non facile puto cuiquam ratione compertum. Sed & eucharistie, seu percipiende seu quo ritu geritur, explicande vel eorum que geruntur in baptismo, verborum, gestorumque, et ordinum, atque interrogationum, et responsionum, quis facile explicet rationem. Et tamen hec omnia operta licet et velata portamus super humeros, quum implemus ea et exequimur, ut a magno pontifice Christo et a filiis eius tradita et commendata suscepimus.*[12] That is to say, but in the observances of the Church are many things which are necessary for us to do, and yet the reason why we do them is not clear to all men. As for example, when we make our prayers kneeling and when, among all the other parts of heaven, we choose the east toward which to make our prayer, I think the reason for this is not easily known to anyone. Also, concerning the observances and the rites we use in the sacrament of the altar to be consecrated, or else the sacrament of baptism to be ministered, who can express the reason for all those words, gestures, orders, questions, answers that are there customary? And yet, nevertheless, all these we bear covered and hid upon our shoulders when we perform and execute them according to the traditions and teachings which we have received recommended to us by the great bishop Christ and by his children the holy apostles. By Origen's words it appears clearly that many such traditions were left to Christian people by Christ and his apostles, traditions which we must follow notwithstanding that they are not written in scripture. To this purpose I might also bring in the testimonies of John Damascene, Augustine, Jerome, and many others.

Thirdly, the third Person of the Trinity, that is to say the Holy Spirit of truth, was sent from the other two to abide with us forever, to be as a continual Comforter in Christ's church when the storms and tempests of heresies should arise, and to teach us against all wavering doubtfulness the very certain truth wherein we should rest. After the apostles were departed from us, the Holy Spirit did and does remain and shall remain with us to the world's end. But by whom, I ask you, does he speak to us? By whom does he teach us any truth? By whom else but by the fathers and doctors of the Church? By their mouths this Holy Spirit teaches us every truth. *Non enim vos estis, qui loquimini, sed Spiritus Patris vestri, qui loquitur in vobis.* That is to say, it is not you who speak, but the Holy Spirit of your Father who speaks within you (Mt 10:20). When Saint Basil was baptized, a wonderful light was seen about him, undoubtedly a sensible token of the Holy Ghost, and likewise while Saint Ambrose was writing on the forty-third psalm, a light was seen above his head in the shape of a shield, which little by little entered in at his mouth in a very token of the Spirit of God. Wherefore it is not to be doubted that in such holy bishops and doctors of the Church the Holy Ghost speaks, and much more in councils when many of them were assembled together. For always when the storms and tempests of heresies arose, so were they at length suppressed and condemned by this Holy Spirit speaking in the mouths of the fathers and doctors of the Church, sometimes by general councils and assemblies of many bishops together. In the Nicene council there were 309 bishops in whom the Holy Ghost spoke to the confutation of a heresy that then sorely vexed the Church. After that, in the council of

Constantinople there were 110 bishops assembled, in whom the Holy Ghost spoke to the destruction of another heresy that then rose in the Church. In the council held in Ephesus, in a great city of Asia so named, were assembled 300 bishops in whom the Holy Spirit then spoke to the confounding of yet another heresy that was aloft. And so, continually from time to time, ever as these clouds arose, made any great tempest, began to cause lightning or show a false light of misconstruing of scriptures, this Holy Spirit was ready by these fathers to inform the universal Church of the certain truth. See then, I say, what we have to confirm those things that are taught us by the Church. First, the prophets that were instructed by the Father almighty God, and also their *cabbala*, that is to say, their secret teachings not written in the Bible. Secondly, the apostles, who were instructed by our Saviour Christ Jesus, and also their traditions not written in the Bible. Thirdly, the holy fathers and doctors of the Church, who were informed by the Holy Spirit of truth, as well in their expositions of scripture as in their general assemblies and councils convened heretofore.

If there were a fourth person in the Trinity, or another spirit to be sent us from almighty God, we might yet be in some doubt whether Martin Luther had met with this spirit by the way and conveyed him from us. But since we are assured that there is no more than three Persons in the godhead, of whom this gospel makes mention, and that every one of them has done his diligence to instruct us in the truth, and since furthermore, there is no other Holy Spirit *preter Spiritum veritatis* but this Spirit of truth who shall abide with us forever and give us assurance of every truth, we may be sure that Martin Luther has not this spirit when he teaches us against the truth that has been taught us by this Spirit. For he cuts away the traditions of the apostles, refuses the general councils, contemns the doctrines of the holy fathers and doctors of the Church, labors to subvert all the ordinance of the Church, namely the seven sacraments, takes away the freedom of man's will, and affirms that all things fall by necessity, contrary to all the doctrine of Christ's Church. We may be sure, therefore, that he has some other wretched spirit, some spirit of error and not the Spirit of truth. Saint Paul says, *in novissimis temporibus discedent quidam a fide, attendentes spiritibus erroris et doctrinis demoniorum.* That is to say, in the latter days of the Church, some shall go from the true faith of Christ's Church and give head to the spirits of error and to the teaching of the devil (1 Tim 4:1). And here note this word *discedent.* For Saint Paul says in another place, *erit discessio primum,* before the coming of Antichrist there shall be a notable discession and departing from the faith of the Church (2 Thess 3). And it is not unlikely that it will be at this time by the occasion of this most perilous heretic.

Here Martin Luther will use his shrewd brain to wrestle with us a bit. He will say that the councils sometimes err and the doctors very often disagree, and since they err and disagree at one time or in one place, so may they do in another, and therefore, he says, he is not bound to believe any of them. To this may be answered that this reasoning will not pass, as I shall make clear. Sometimes when the prophets were left to themselves, they deviated from the truth: *nam prophetie spiritus non semper prophetarum mentes irradiat,* the spirit of prophecy does not always shine bright upon the minds of the prophets. For example, when King David planned to build the temple to almighty God and took counsel of the prophet Nathan whether he should perform his purpose yes or no, the prophet Nathan told him to go ahead with it and do all that he intended in his heart to do, *omnia que in corde tuo sunt fac, dominus tecum est.* That is, do all that you intend in your heart, for our Lord God is with you (2 Sam 7:3). Yet he was deceived, for it was not as he said. Shall we now for this mistake trust nothing else this prophet Nathan said? God forbid. Likewise of the apostles: when Saint Peter said to Christ, *Tu es Christus, Filius Dei vivi,* Thou art Christ, the Son of the living God, he spoke this by revelation, and here our Savior praised him and said, *beatus es Petrus Bar Jona,* thou art blessed, Peter son of Jonah (Mt 16:16-7). Within a little while he dissuaded our Savior from his passion and said, *absit a te, Domine,* not so, good Lord, and in this he spoke wrongly (Mt 16:22). Now, because he spoke wrongly the second time, shall we not believe his first saying? That would not be reasonable. Almighty God permitted the prophets and also the apostles to err sometimes so that we might know they were only men. When they said the truth, they had it of God, but when they said otherwise than the truth, it came of themselves. Therefore, we shall not deny them generally, nor the councils. Even if one of the last councils, which was perhaps not gathered in the meekness and charity that was expedient, had been permitted to go amiss (something which I will not affirm), should we therefore damn all the rest? It would not be reasonable. And this may suffice for the third instruction.

The Fourth Instruction:
the Defence Made by Luther's Adherents

The fourth and final instruction takes away the defence that is made for Martin Luther by his adherents, a defence that can also quickly overthrow weak souls when they hear it. Their defence consists of three points. First, they say that Martin Luther is a man who is deeply learned in the scriptures and grounds all his opinions upon them and a man of religious life, who for his learning and virtue has many adherents. Secondly, they say that he has a mind fixed on God and does not allow any man's authority to keep him from speaking the truth. So much so that he has excommunicated the pope, for he thinks in his own conscience that those who do not follow his doctrine are not of the Catholic Church. Thirdly, he has a marvellously fervent zeal towards God, which makes him labor to convert all the world to his opinion, thinking assuredly by this to do a special sacrifice and be pleasing to God. When a weak soul hears this defence, he is immediately in danger of giving faith to it and of mistrusting the doctrine of the Church. For who can think that such a man is not in the right way? But then the rest of the gospel that ensues answers this clearly. It follows, *hec locutus sum vobis, ut non scandalizemini. Absque synagogis facient vos; sed venit hora, ut omnis, qui interficit vos, arbitretur obsequium se prestare Deo.*

That is to say, this I have told you beforehand, so that you shall not quail in your faith; for they shall divide you from their synagogues, and the time shall come when every man that murders you shall think he does thereby a great service to God (Jn 16:1-2). Some may think these words pertain only to the time of the Jews, who expelled the apostles from their synagogues, or to the time of the tyrants, who slew many Christians at the beginning of the Church. But if that were true, then these words would not be a general instruction for the Universal Church, which is something we concluded against Luther at the beginning of our sermon. Wherefore, much rather do these words pertain to the times of the heretics. First, because their persecution continued longer than the other two, for the persecution of the Jews was soon ended, and the persecution of the tyrants had its course for a season, but the heretics have persecuted the Church since the Ascension of Christ and shall do so until the coming of Antichrist. Furthermore, the persecution of the heretics is and always was more perilous than the other two, for the Jews and the tyrants were manifest enemies of Christ and abhorred his scriptures, but these heretics pretend a special regard for Christ and color all their heresies with his scriptures. When the Jews and the tyrants slew the bodies of Christian men, they sent their souls to everlasting glory, but when the heretics misconstrued the scriptures of God by their false doctrine, erroneous opinions, and pestilent heresies, they slew the souls of Christian people and sent them to everlasting damnation. Wherefore these words must rather be understood of the persecution that was made by the heretics. Now then, Christian man, when you hear that Martin Luther is a man of great learning, has great skill with scriptures, is reputed to be of virtuous living, and has many great adherents, think that there have been many such before him in the Church of Christ. By their learning and mistaking of scriptures, many others have made such tempests in the Church before this time.

What a tempest did the great heretic Arius raise in the Church of Christ by his heresy, and what a great murder of souls did he make! Was he not a man of great learning, of singular eloquence, of virtuous life in outward appearance? He grounded all his opinions upon scripture and so deceived many a soul. Saint Jerome says, *Arrius una scintilla in Alexandria fuit, sed quia non cito extincta est, totum orbem populata est flamma eius.*[13] That is to say, in the city of Alexandria, Arius was only one spark, but because this spark was not quenched quickly, the flame that rose from it raged throughout the world. It vexed the Church of Christ a long time and overthrew innumerable souls, till at length the Holy Spirit of truth, the Comforter of Christ's Church, spoke, as I said before, by the mouths of the fathers and doctors of the Church, so that this heresy was condemned and plainly put aside.

But after this tempest immediately rose up another cloud called Macedonius, who likewise vexed the Church, and after him Nestorius, after him Eutyches, and so forth, storm after storm, one upon another. So that as soon as one storm was pacified, the wicked spirits raised up another without a pause. Saint Augustine remembers 57 capital heresies since the Ascension of Christ, that rose at different times like so many clouds and storms in the Church, to be finally condemned by the Holy Spirit of truth.[14] And every one of these heretics grounded his heresy upon scripture, and many of them were men of keen wit, deep learning, mighty reasoning, and pretended virtue, and had the distinctive ability to wrest and distort the scriptures, to make them appear to be on the side of their erroneous opinions. And finally, their manner of life, learning, and handling of scriptures were such that they had many great adherents and favorers, as well among bishops as among emperors and other Christian princes, also, who were abused by them. Therefore, it was necessary that our Savior Christ Jesus, because of his great, inestimable goodness and the tender love he bears his Church, should leave an instruction and warning to all Christian people and to his Universal Church about this persecution. And so he did, saying, *hec locutus sum vobis, ut non scandalizemini.* I have told you, says he, these things beforehand so that you shall not quail in your faith. What has he told us beforehand? This: that the Spirit of truth shall remain in the Church forever and that in all such storms and tempests he shall be a Comforter to us. O Christian man, hear this gracious warning of our Savior Christ. Mark well what he says: I have warned you, says he, of these things beforehand, because then, when they happen, you shall not be overthrown in your souls by them. It is as though he said: when you shall see the storms arise, when you shall behold the thick, black clouds aloft darkening all the face of the heavens, shadowing from you the clear light of the sun, showing a false, glistering light that issues out of the cloud from the spirit of the tempest, and when you shall hear the terrible threat of their thundering, be then constant in your faith. Believe as does your mother holy Church in a lively manner, and put your trust in the Spirit of truth, who shall be your Comforter to the world's end.

Furthermore, when you hear, Christian man, that Martin Luther has a mind fixed on God, that he does not for any man's authority refrain from speaking the truth, and that he reputes all those who do not follow his doctrine to be divided from the Catholic Church, so much so that he has excommunicated the pope—O wonderful presumption, O madness intolerable—know this for certain, that all the other heretics did thus. They reputed only themselves and their adherents to be of the Catholic Church and regarded all the others who followed not their opinions as being divided from the Church. So did the Novatians in Rome exclude the Catholic priests and bishops from their Churches. So did the Arians likewise in Greece. So did the Donatists in Africa. Nevertheless, the Church of Christ is but one, *una, sancta, catholica, et apostolica*. This Church is one, having one head, the pope, who is the vicar of Christ, from whom it is called *una*. And though there are many sinners in this Church, yet because the holy sacraments renew and repair sinners daily and because the Holy Spirit continually remains in it, it is called *sancta*, that is to say, holy. And because it is not limited to any particular nation, but common to all nations, therefore it is called *catholica*, that is to say, universal.

And finally, because it is derived from the apostles and especially from the prince of the apostles Saint Peter, therefore it is called *apostolica*, that is to say, apostolic. This Church alone is the spouse of Christ; all others that resemble it but are not of this Church are synagogues of Satan and assemblies of the devil. And therefore, Christian man, do not be astonished even if they excommunicate and divide true Christians from their synagogues. For our Savior has given us warning of this beforehand, saying as it follows in the gospel, *absque synagogis facient vos*, that is to say, they shall excommunicate you and divide you from their synagogues. Thirdly, Christian man, when you hear that Martin Luther has so great a zeal for God that he thinks himself in his conscience bound to do as he does, that he thinks he pleases God, does a special service to God, and recommits to almighty God all the souls he slays and murders by his false doctrine, yet nevertheless, be strong in your faith, and see that in this point also our Savior has warned the Church, saying, *sed venit hora, quando omnis qui interficit vos, arbitretur obsequium se prestare Deo*. That is to say, the time comes when every man that shall murder you shall think that he does acceptable service to God. If the other heretics had not done thus before, then you might think that Martin Luther is remarkable. But did not the Arians do thus? Did they not furiously rage against the Catholic bishops and priests who resisted them? Not only did they infect the souls of men by their pestilent errors, they also caused great murders of bodies. Did not the Donatists act thus, of whom Saint Augustine speaks to Boniface, *quicunque dura illorum verba contempserant, durioribus verberibus quod iubebant facere cogebantur; innocentium qui eos offenderant domus, aut deponebantur ad solum, aut ignibus cremabantur*.[15] That is to say, those who disregarded their hard words (*verba*) were constrained with harder strokes (*verberibus*) to follow their will; the houses of good Christians were razed to the ground or set on fire. And after this follows, *quod plurimi cedibus eorum extincti sunt*, that is to say, many were killed by them. Did not the disciples of Wycliff do the same? Although for fear of the temporal laws they did not dare kill any man themselves, yet they put up a bill of articles to the temporal lords in parliament season [1395], to move them to slay their adversaries who resisted them. And what do you suppose Martin Luther and his adherents would do if they had power over the pope's holiness and his favorers, those he calls so often in derision *papistas, papastros, papanos, and papenses*? I fear he would use no more courtesy with them than he has done with their books, that is to say, with the decretals he has burned. So likewise, I fear, he would burn them or any other Christian man he thought could prevent his opinions from going forward. And yet in so doing he would think he did great service to God.

Thus, you may see that these heretics, even though they had great dexterity with scriptures, were keen of wit and deep of reasoning, led a seemingly virtuous life, showed great zeal, and thought in their conscience that they were bound to do as much as they did, yet they were deceived, and by the holy councils and fathers of the Church they were condemned for their erroneous opinions. And why may not Martin Luther be deceived likewise, as they all were before him? And especially since he lacks the Spirit of truth, the one they all lacked. For if they had had the Spirit of truth, they would not have erred in misconceiving the scriptures. I admit they were dexterous in handling scriptures, could bring them marvellously to their purpose, and frame them cursedly to their opinions. But for lack of the Spirit of truth, they misconstrued these scriptures, as Saint Peter says, *depravabant*, or as Saint Paul says, *invertebant* (2 Pt 3:16; Gal 1:7). They turned the wrong side of the scriptures outward, following their own brain and fantasy, led by the spirit of error and ignorance, as it follows: *hec omnia facient vobis, quia non noverunt Patrem neque me* (Jn 16:3). That is to say, all this they shall do unto you because they know not my Father, nor me. If they had had the Spirit of truth, this Spirit would have led them to the true knowledge of the Father and of the Son, that is to say, to the true knowledge of the prophets by whom almighty God the Father spoke and to the true knowledge also of the apostles by whom the Son our Savior Christ

Jesus spoke. But because they had not this Spirit of truth sent from the Father and from the Son, therefore they were ignorant of them both. And by that ignorance they fell into these misfortunes. And so likewise has Martin Luther now done.

Recapitulation

Now then, here I make an end. I have reminded you, according to my promise, of four instructions that are graciously offered us in this gospel. First, that the Holy Spirit, who is the third Person in the divinity, was sent from the Father almighty God and from his Son our Savior Christ Jesus, to be the Spirit of truth, abiding forever in the Church of Christ to be as a Comforter from time to time against all storms and tempests of heresies, giving us in every time of doubtfulness assurance of the very truth which we should hold and keep. By occasion of this instruction I showed three things. First, that this instruction and the whole gospel pertains to the Universal Church of Christ, something I proved by Luther's own words. Secondly, that the head of this Universal Church is the pope, under Christ, which one point takes away one great ground of Martin Luther and sorely shakes many of his erroneous articles. Thirdly, that by dividing himself from the head of this body, Martin Luther cannot have in him this Spirit of truth. For the second instruction, I showed that the heat of charity spread in our hearts by the Holy Spirit of God gives evidence of the lively light of faith shining upon our souls from our Savior Christ. By this instruction another great ground of Martin Luther's was undermined, which is that faith alone, without works, justifies a sinner. For the third instruction, I showed that the teachings left to the Church by the holy apostles bear testimony to us of the faith of Christ, of the things we shall believe in his Church. Here also was lost another ground of Martin Luther, who will not admit any other testimony but what is written in scripture. Against him I proved that, besides the written scriptures, he must receive the unwritten traditions of the apostles, the general councils in whom the Holy Ghost spoke, and the interpretations of scriptures made by the holy bishops and doctors of the Church, by whose mouths the third Person in the godhead, the Spirit of truth spoke and speaks, informing the Church for this time as the Father almighty God did before by his prophets, and as his Son the second Person did by his apostles. For the fourth instruction, I showed you that the defence made for Martin Luther by his adherents, whereby many weak souls are overthrown, is clearly taken away by the most loving and most gracious forewarning of our Savior Christ, as you have heard at the end of the gospel. And yet again, because of his most excellent charity, he warns all his Christian people, saying and repeating, *hec locutus sum vobis, ut cum venerit hora eorum, reminiscamini eorum, quia ego dixi vobis* (Jn 16:4). That is to say, these things I have told you, so that when the dangers shall happen, you may remember that I warned you of them beforehand. Who after so many warnings will still give faith to Martin Luther or to any such heretic, rather than to Christ Jesus and to the Spirit of truth who abides in the Church of Christ to the world's end to inform us of the truth? This man goes far wide from the straight way and is never likely to enter into the port of everlasting rest which we all desire and yearn to come to, to which may he bring us, *qui cum Patre et Spiritu Sancto vivet et regnat Deus per omnia secula seculorum. Amen.*

Notes

[1] St. Augustine, *Liber quaestionum de Novo et Veteri Testamento*, Migne PL, vol. 35, col. 2269-70.

[2] The passage (in Migne PL, vol. 39, col. 2102) is part of a spurious sermon of St. Augustine, which in Fisher's time was still attributed to St. Ambrose. As Mgr. Hallett noted in the Preface to his translation, some of Fisher's quotations from the Fathers, which he often gives without any reference, are difficult to trace. Most of Fisher's quotations are remarkably precise.

[3] St. Gregory, Letter to John, bishop of Constantinople, in Migne PL, vol. 77, col. 740.

4 The quotation is from St. Jerome's *Adversus Jovinianum* (lib. 1), in Migne PL, vol. 23, col. 258.

5 St. Cyprian, epistola 69, in Migne PL, vol. 4, col. 418.

6 St. Chrysostome, *Homiliae in Joannem,* Hom. 88, in Migne PG, vol. 59, col. 478.

7 Origen, *In Exodum*, Homilia 5, in Migne PG, vol. 12, col. 329.

8 Henry VIII's book defending the sacraments against Luther was entitled, *Assertio septem Sacramentorum adversus Martinum Lutherum, edita ab invictissimo Angliae et Franciae rege, et domino Hiberniae, Henrico ejus nominis octavo* (London, 1521). Henry VIII wrote the book in order to obtain a title similar to the one, "Christianissimus," already enjoyed by the French King, Louis XII. As recounted by J. J. Scarisbrick in his *Henry VIII* (London: Eyre & Spottiswoode, 1968, pp. 115-17), Rome granted the title "Defensor Fidei" only after considerable hesitation. Henry's hankering for such a title was motivated not so much by his interest in orthodoxy, as by his wish to raise his international stature and by his resolve to build up among his subjects an excessive adulation of the royal office. In the latter respect, as events were to show, he certainly succeeded. The title given to Henry was not meant to be hereditary, but, as it happened with all such titles, they were eagerly claimed by the successors of the recipient. As reported by John Lingard in his monumental *History of England* (London: J. C. Nimmo & Bain, 1883), vol. 4, pp. 467-68, it was believed that John Fisher had had a hand in collecting the materials for the book, which the king himself composed, though with a result that hardly passes for a significant theological treatise. An edition that contains the Latin text of Henry's *Assertio* together with an English translation in parallel pages was published by L. O'Donovan (New York: Benziger Brothers, 1908), with a valuable introduction.

9 Plato, *Republic*, 5:473c-d.

10 *De fide et operibus,* cap. xiv, in Migne PL, vol. 40, col. 211. At that time this work was still believed to have been written by St. Augustine.

11 According to the *Oxford English Dictionary*, the word *cabbala* derives from the Hebrew *quabbalah*, and was originally the name given in post-biblical Hebrew to the oral tradition handed down and recorded in the Mishnah and Talmud. The first example given in the *Oxford English Dictionary* is this passage in John Fisher's Sermon against Luther.

12 Origen, *Homiliae super librum Numerorum,* Hom. 5, in Migne PG, vol. 12, col. 603.

[13] St. Jerome, *Commentarius in epistolam ad Galatas*, in Migne PL, vol. 26, col. 403.
[14] St. Augustine, *De haeresibus liber unus*, in Migne PL, vol. 42, col. 24-25.
[15] St. Augustine, *Epistula ad Bonifacium* (a long letter also known as *De correctione Donatistarum liber*), in Migne PL, vol. 33, col. 799.